RED & YELLOW, BLACK & WHITE...

RED & YELLOW, BLACK & WHITE...

Deborah Sue Brunsman

COLLEGE PRESS PUBLISHING COMPANY
Joplin,Missouri

Printed and Bound in the
United States of America
All Rights Reserved

Library of Congress Catalog Card Number 90-86284
International Standard Book Number: 0-89900-385-0

DEDICATED

To my Mother and Dad,
the late Joanne B. Brunsman
and Richard S. Brunsman
with love and appreciation

TABLE OF CONTENTS

LIST OF ILLUSTRATIONS

FOREWORD

Today's surprise is that reaching the nations of the world has become "easier" for those of us who live in the USA. People from many ethnic backgrounds have come to us. We don't have to cross so many geographic borders to allow many from other nations to hear the message.

However, the "cultural" borders remain. People from all over the world have journeyed to the USA and become Americans, but they do not lose their cultural distinctives. Even though they live in the USA, their first language is not English and their culture is not predominantly Anglo-American.

The author, herself a successful East Coast missionary to non-Anglo ethnic groups, encourages us to cross these cultural borders because Jesus would want us to.

This cross-cultural ministry is not all easy but it is possible. It has been done many times already. Christian leaders have called this one of the latest sharp edges of ministry, yet there are still many who are unfamiliar with this mission. This book makes us aware of the vast need for mission to the great variety of ethnic peoples who are often overlooked. These words are written to encourage believers in Jesus to follow His words about making disciples.

Many from various ethnic groups who are already disciples have the vision to make followers of Jesus among their own peoples. And they are doing it. Often among the most recent immigrants – and hence the poorest – they take the opportunity to help others get settled in the USA and also share Jesus. Few groups have the luxury of full-time ministers, yet they still plant churches and train new leaders.

Sometimes, multi-cultural churches are being formed, which must give us a sampling of the universal heavenly culture – not a celestial melting pot but a rich variety of people expressing their praise to God. More often, a distinct ethnic group desires to have its own church, where Christians can worship in their first language and with cultural patterns which are familiar and comfortable to them. Multi-cultural mission welcomes and encourages this.

However, to wait for the various ethnic groups to bring the message of Jesus to their own people is impractical. There is not enough time. Many cultural groups have very few Christians among them. They come from countries which were completely unreached before. The leaders themselves may have come to Christ as refugees in a third country or through the love of a friend in the USA.

In this book, Anglo-American Christians are especially called to heed this commission to mission. As a part of the dominant culture, they have many advantages and are often eagerly accepted by newer arriving ethnic groups. They must be good managers of their responsibilities.

Yet Christians from non-Anglo backgrounds also need to move cross-culturally. They may be extremely effective in mission; for example, Filipinos to Indonesians, African-Americans to Zimbabweans, Koreans to Japanese. Non-Christian Anglo-Americans need to be nudged off-balance for a fresh look at the message of Jesus. It may be that a former Buddhist or Muslim from another cultural background will do that as well as another Anglo-American.

Some will suggest that we wait until the various ethnic groups become absorbed into the dominant Anglo-American culture when they will be easier to reach. Two reasons quickly abolish this counsel. First, the melting pot theory has not come to pass. People are retaining strong elements of their first culture for a much longer time than in the earliest days of immigration. It will not work.

Secondly, as non-Anglo Americans come closer to the dominant culture, they actually become more unreachable. They are fascinated with the primary elements of American culture, like consumerism, individualism and scientism, which take them further from the message of Jesus. Exotic as it sounds, their former culture may make them more open to Jesus than their

American experience.

Those with experience explain that there is only a small window of time when new immigrants are most reachable. If they are befriended and shown a richer way of life in Jesus, it may have eternal consequences. To wait is to risk not reaching them at all.

The author's message does not blunt the need for people to do traditional overseas mission. That is still needed, but the book shows us a mission field which is hidden to many people, even though we may be looking at it every day. Read it with one eye open to God and another eye open to people of another culture whom God loves.

Dr. Roger Edrington
Director, Multi-Cultural Missions
San Jose (CA) Christian College

ACKNOWLEDGMENTS

I wish to thank Chris DeWelt of the College Press Publishing Company in Joplin, Missouri who had the vision for the need of a book on reaching the ethnic communities in America and encouraged me in the task of writing this work. I would also like to thank Dr. Roger Edrington of the Multi-Cultural Missions Department at San Jose Christian College in San Jose, California, who read the draft manuscript of this book and offered valuable suggestions and comments that proved helpful in the preparation of this present volume.

Deborah Sue Brunsman
September, 1990

INTRODUCTION

In New York Harbor stands a colossal statue with arms stretched wide open. On this Statue of Liberty an invitation to the world is inscribed:

Give me your tired, your poor,
Your huddled masses yearning to breathe free,
The wretched refuse of your teeming shore,
Send these, the homeless, tempest-tossed to me.

For over one hundred years the Lady has offered freedom and a new way of life to countless millions who have sought refuge on her shores. For decades the eyes of the world have looked to her to come here. Liberal immigration laws have made the United States the magnet of the world. For the last half century America has drawn immigrants in ever-increasing numbers so that today over fifty percent of the United States populace are people with ethnic, racial, language, and cultural identities other than Anglo-American. This nation has become more diverse than ever before.

Walk this nation's streets, and a Christian finds peoples of all colors, languages, smells, and cultures. Teeming multitudes of humanity, speaking every language and representing every nationality, race, and religion, have been arriving on America's shores each year. These recognizable ethnic groups throughout the country demonstrate the undeniable reality that we live in a multi-cultural society.

Although the Anglo-Saxon culture maintains a predominate influence in America, especially with the English language, the melting pot that was to bring cultural homogeneity has not happened. America, instead, is like a stew pot of various ingredients, with each ethnic group changing and enriching each other while maintaining its own identity and integrity.

The beacon of liberty from the Lady has brought an ethnic mosaic into America's midst, and this fact offers the Anglo-American church a new and exciting challenge to fulfill the Great Commission. While the mission field is still overseas, it has moved to America also.

For decades children in the Anglo-American church have been singing: "Red and Yellow, Black and White, They Are Precious in His Sight; Jesus Loves the Little Children of the World." Every generation of Christians is faced with new challenges, and one of the greatest challenges for this generation is to learn to relate the gospel of Jesus' love effectively across cultural differences and in urban settings to these "red and yellow, black andwhite" who are arriving at America's doorstep. How Anglo-Americans face the "red and yellow, black and white" of this multi-ethnic nation and how Anglo-American Christians evangelize other ethnic peoples is of major significance.

What God is doing in bringing this potpourri of peoples to America is one of the great dramas in human history. Never in the history of the Christian church has a generation of Christians had a greater opportunity to reach the peoples of the world than exists in the United States today. Ethnic peoples from most nations and cultural groups to which churches in the United States have sent missionaries and mission dollars for decades are visiting or immigrating to America in unprecedented numbers. As a result, the United States has become one of the largest multi-cultural, multi-ethnic nations in the history of the world.

Ethnics are defined as those people who see themselves as different from the dominant culture because of language, national origin, or religious tradition. Even though Anglo-Saxon Americans constitute an ethnic group of people with a common language and heritage and are a minority in the world's population, they are the standard culture in the United States by which all ethnic languages, cultures, and customs are measured. Ethnic groups in America are considered to be those who are non-Anglo and are distinct from the prevailing Anglo-Saxon norm.

Sadly, most of these non-Anglo ethnics have remained virtually untouched by the evangelistic outreach of the Anglo-American church and isolated from the gospel message. For years churches have been growing and multiplying particularly among Anglo-Americans, but not among many of the other ethnic groups. Anglo-American Christians have failed to reach ethnic America – neglecting the Biblical mandate, giving way to fears, and lingering in provincialism. Since the Christian faith is not limited to one language or culture, the Anglo-American church cannot honestly speak about evangelizing this great country without considering this mixture of ethnic groups.

This book is written primarily to help Anglo-American Christians, the dominant ethnic group, to recognize that the non-Anglo segments of this multi-cultural society now constitute the majority of the American population. The desire of the author is to help the reader to overcome the hindrances which keep Anglo-American Christians from reaching the potpourri of peoples in this multi-cultural nation with the gospel and to offer suggestions for launching outreach ministries to the various non-Anglo ethnic populations in their midst.

Part I describes the changing face of America, with its ever-increasing diversity and complexity, and the challenge which America's ethnicity brings to the Anglo church as she proclaims the gospel. Part II includes a discussion of three stumbling blocks – indifference, fears, and provincialism – which impair the Anglo-American church's ability to acknowledge the ethnic presence in America and to reach it with the reconciling message of the cross. Part III offers several practical suggestions which Christians and churches may use in beginning evangelistic ministries to the lost among America's non-Anglo ethnic population and discusses the commitment which is needed to maintain vibrant ethnic ministries into the Twenty-first Century.

The thesis of this book is that every individual, regardless of language, culture, racial, or ethnic background, should have the opportunity to discover salvation in Jesus Christ and to worship God in a language and culture with which he is most familiar and comfortable. Unless the Anglo church in the United States reaches out to non-Anglo peoples, segments of America's communities will not hear the gospel nor have the opportunity to know God as their Savior and Lord.

Anglo-American Christians must concentrate on the evangelization of other ethnic populations in this country while they are reachable. Many non-Anglo people will live and die in Christian America having been insulated from hearing the good news of Christ because of language or culture, sometimes within eyesight of a Anglo-American church or even after having lived next door to a believer.ß Anglo-American Christians must initiate evangelistic programs which target these unchurched segments of society.

The church dare not bypass the spiritual needs of those in its neighborhoods. The love of Christ compels Anglo-American Christians to reach out to the rainbow of peoples who are a part of this multi-cultural nation so that these millions may find refuge in the Savior. May the readers of this book become a part of the committed ambassadors of Christ who have realized that America is a mosaic and have become ministers for Christ to the "red and yellow, black and white" within the borders of this nation.

PART ONE

THE ETHNIC MOSAIC AT AMERICA'S DOORSTEP

THE CHANGING FACE OF AMERICA

The land that drew the world's tired, poor, huddled masses like a magnet has become a mosaic of people whose heritage represents over two hundred language and culture groups. For decades peoples from the mission fields of the world have been coming to America. Wave upon wave of immigrants – thousands, millions, and more – year after year, have been arriving on these American shores.

Repeal of the Immigration Act of 1965 opened the floodgates to an unprecedented migration of peoples by eliminating the national quotas and opening the way for a great increase in immigrants, especially from Asia and the Middle East.[1] These liberal immigration laws made the United States the destination for thousands of people from all over the world. As a result, for the last sixty years America has drawn immigrants, refugees, and undocumented aliens in ever-increasing numbers so that today the majority of the United States populace are people with ethnic, language, and cultural identities other than Anglo-American.

Walk the streets of American cities and a person visits the world. Scores of distinct nationalities concentrated in cities and towns across America bear witness to the fact that this country is changing from a dominant Anglo-Saxon society to a multi-ethnic, multinational mingling of peoples from the world. The recognizable ethnic groups throughout the country demonstrate this undeniable reality. With over fifty percent of this nation's population identifying with an ethnic group other than Anglo-American, the mission field has been placed on the nation's doorstep.

THE WORLD IS HERE

The history of America has been the story of a nation of ethnics. When America was born, Europeans abandoned their traditional cultures, braved the Atlantic Ocean to start a new life, and fused together into the predominant Anglo-Saxon culture. Indians, Africans, and Orientals also contributed to the development of this new nation; yet, they retained many of their ethnic qualities while establishing new traditions unique to America. Over the centuries, a massive stream of humanity crossed every ocean and continent to reach the United States.

Each new immigrant settled into a society of American ethnics, contributing a part of their ethnic culture to the whole. Every fiber of this developing nation's life – music, arts, law, medicine, science, education, and politics – was touched and influenced by ethnic people. Everyone made unique contributions and added great strengths to the American society, infusing it with talent and energy.[2]

With later waves of immigration the face of America changed even more. Older immigrants faded into the mainstream of American society, while new immigrants appeared from entirely new areas to begin again the drama of the peopling of America. During the Twentieth Century, however, the majority of new immigrants no longer came from Europe. For the first time in the history of the nation, more than half the new immigrants came from Asia and Latin America. The ethnic population surged as millions were admitted legally, with perhaps millions more entering illegally.

By the end of the eighties, millions of foreigners were being added annually to the ethnic composition of the country. Over half of the entire population of the United States considered themselves non-Anglo ethnics, with Anglo-Americans making up less then one-third of the American population. The other two-thirds were composed of more than two hundred ethnic groups, communicating in over five hundred distinct languages and dialects. Non-Anglo ethnics were increasing. The face of America was changing.

AMERICA IS AN ETHNIC MOSAIC

Until the decade of the sixties, most Americans

thought of the United States as a melting pot where all cultures were fused into the one dominant Anglo-American culture. In the minds of most American people of that time, ethnic cultures were at best a nuisance to be tolerated by society.

Fig. 1. U.S. Population from Ethnic, Language, and Culture Backgrounds Other Than Anglo-American

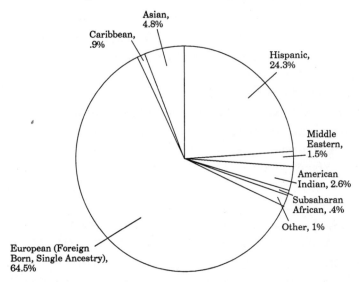

The upheaval of the sixties, however, forced Americans to recognize that this nation was not a melting pot and never had been. In reality, the United States was a pluralistic nation with numerous and diverse cultures and languages which held unique characteristics. Americans began trading the melting pot view of our society for that of a many-colored mosaic, interwoven with a variety of peoples of all races, nationalities, and cultures.[3]

26

Multitudes of ethnics, upon arriving in America, had not left behind their personal beliefs and cultural backgrounds. They had not abandoned their value systems, social patterns, art forms, nor traditions. They remained linked by tradition, religion, language, history, and racial distinction which contributed to their perception of being a part of a culture other than the dominant Anglo-Saxon culture.[4]

These peoples maintained their distinct ethnic identity and solidarity. Many of these ethnics spoke a language other than English; others spoke English but had a different cultural heritage than Anglo-American. Many ethnic groups were regarded as minority cultures within the American social system, even though in the broadest sense of the term all Americans, including Anglo-Americans, could be considered ethnics by virtue of being descendants of immigrants.

THE FACE OF AMERICA IS STILL CHANGING

In the nineties, however, non-Anglo ethnic Americans can no longer be considered the minority in the United States. Ethnic groups other than Anglo-Americans now make up the majority of people in our country and are likely to increase disproportionately as the years go by. Increased immigration and higher birth rates among non-Anglos have boosted the nation's ethnic population and will continue to play a significant role in the growth of ethnic America. This numerical gain among ethnics has made the diversity of American's population increasingly more noticeable.[5]

American society is radically more pluralistic and is shifting in perspective and cultural heritage. While historically America received its immigrants from Europe, today approximately eighty percent of all immigrants are from Asian or Latin American nations. Two out of five immigrants are now Asian, making it the fastest growing ethnic group in the country.[6] One American in twelve is Hispanic, and the proportion of Hispanics is expanding rapidly, out-pacing the rest of the population five to one.[7]

The real America of the nineties is an increasingly complex mixture of many ethnic groups, each contributing to the multi-cultural, multi-ethnic fabric of the nation. The United States now has the distinction of being the largest Jewish nation in the world, the second largest Polish nation, and the fourth largest Spanish-speaking nation. More people of Irish ancestry live in the United States than in Ireland, and more African-Americans than in most African countries. Twenty percent of the populace uses a language other than English, and daily newspapers are printed in more than forty-five different languages in this country. All of this indicates that the ethnic mosaic is intact and that the ethnic populations are enormous in size and growing.

The changing face of America is most evident in the nation's cities. Regardless of what major American city one lives in, the people of the world are all around. The projection is that by the year 2000, more than fifty major American cities will be predominantly made up of ethnic groups other than Anglo-American. New York City, the original ethnic metropolis, is becoming increasingly non-Anglo. The older immigrants still hold their own in traditional ethnic neighborhoods, but new faces are turning up in the city, transforming its communities.

New York City is the second largest Puerto Rican city in the world, after San Juan. This metropolitan area is the fourth largest Italian city, following Rome, Milan, and Naples; the third largest Greek community in the world resides within its borders. Currently one in every three New Yorkers is foreign born, and projections are that this will increase to one in every two by the end of the century.

Although New York remains a vibrant immigrant city, she is no longer the gateway to America. The ethnic settlement of contemporary America has shifted South and West to Los Angeles and Texas. During the past two decades one in five immigrants has settled in Los Angeles. Los Angeles has become like a booming Third World city, earning the distinction of being the second largest Korean city in the world, the second largest Hispanic city in the Western Hemisphere, and the Vietnamese capital of America.

Because Los Angeles has become the destination for people from other countries, its urban borders swell with a variety of ethnic languages and cultures. Students in the Los Angeles Unified School District speak over one hundred languages, with pupils of Spanish, Korean, Vietnamese, Cantonese, and Armenian descent numbering in the thousands. City police in Los Angeles speak a total of forty-two languages.

Scores of other cities in America are experiencing the burgeoning of this nation's ethnic population. Regardless of what major American city a person may dwell in, the people of the world are all around. Chicago is the second largest Polish city in the world, Miami the second largest Cuban city, and Brooklyn the second largest Haitian city. Detroit's ethnic diversity makes it home to the largest Arab population in America with over 250,000 of Arabian ancestry. Hispanics make up the majority of the populace in El Paso and San Antonio, and the Minneapolis-St. Paul metropolitan area contains a major Laotian community. Nearly ninety percent of recent immigrants live in one of America's metropolitan areas.

Naturally, America's states are feeling the impact of the ethnic growth. Along the Rio Grande, Spanish is the language of preference, while elsewhere in Texas Asians are transforming neighborhoods and taking over businesses. In New Mexico over twenty-five percent of the people are Spanish-speaking. American Indians are now outnumbered by Hispanics in Utah. French Americans comprise one-third of Maine's population. The State of Michigan is home to over one-quarter million Arabs, and many of its public schools recognize Muslim holy days and refrain from serving pork in the cafeterias. Because of the rapid increase in California's Hispanic population, before the turn of the century California could once again be a Spanish-speaking state.

By the thousands, peoples from around the world – immigrants, refugees, students, tourists, diplomats, businessmen – have been transplanted in the United States. America has become a rainbow of colors, languages, and cultural traditions. The recognizable ethnic groups throughout the country demonstrate the undeniable reality that the face of America is still changing. America is a mosaic.

THE CHALLENGE TO AMERICA'S CHURCH

The visibility of ethnic groups throughout the nation testifies to an indisputable fact that the world is at the doorstep of the American church. This truth offers the church a new and exciting challenge to fulfill the Great Commission. While the mission field is still overseas, it has moved to America also. Since millions of unreached peoples have been placed in America's backyard, the Anglo-American church must strive with urgency to reach out to the mixture of ethnic groups in America with Jesus' love.

Most of the newly arriving immigrants are from cultural groups formerly beyond the reach of the missions and churches of North America, providing the church with opportunities to share the gospel cross-culturally right at home. Most Anglo-American Christians cannot go to the grocery store without being surrounded by opportunities for ethnic evangelism.

Although unreached peoples of the world have come to America in unprecedented numbers, they remain nearly as unevangelized in the United States as they were in their native countries. Although some evangelistic concern by the Anglo-American church has produced ethnic ministries and churches in the United States which worship in languages other than English, many evangelistic efforts which have been attempted among ethnic communities have been small and poorly funded. Frequently, ethnics have been required to assimilate into the Anglo-American culture to be saved, individuals from outside the ethnic community have led ethnic churches, and endeavors to train non-Anglos to reach their own group with the gospel have been minimal.

Estimates indicate that less than one-half of one percent of all ethnics in this nation are being reached by the gospel witness of Anglo-American churches.[8] When statistics of unchurched ethnics in this country are compared to the mission populations of other nations, America has become one of the larger mission fields needing the gospel.

Anglo-American Christians need to recognize the changing face of America, acknowledge the mission potential in the ethnic mosaic, and concentrate on the evangelization of other ethnic populations in this country while they are reachable. The final frontier of evangelism in this nation is ethnic America.

Nevertheless, while the world literally has come to America, this nation's Anglo-American Christians continue to expend tremendous resources in overseas missions to the neglect of the receptive ethnic populations in the United States. These unreached segments of our society stand in the shadows of many churches, being ignored as one of the most receptive mission fields of the world. Newly arriving immigrants, who are most reachable during their first eighteen months of residence,[9] have been overlooked by the church for years and now many show little interest in the gospel.

With such a large percentage of non-Anglo peoples being unevangelized, it is urgent that Anglo-American Christians direct more cross-cultural efforts toward the pockets of ethnics living in the United States who are essentially beyond the sound of the gospel. Simply proclaiming that the church is open to everyone, regardless of language or cultural differences, is not sufficient. The church in America must awaken, must regard itself as being in a truly mission situation, and must meet the spiritual needs of those in its community through a cross-cultural proclamation of the gospel.

The face of America has changed. Millions of ethnic peoples from one hundred and fifty countries reside in America, leaving the Anglo-American church in the United States with the unique opportunity to literally touch the world with the gospel. Let the Anglo-American church rise to this challenge and concentrate on the evangelization of America's multi-cultural population while it can be reached.

Endnotes

1. William Broyles, Jr. "Promise of America," *U.S. News and World Report,* 7 July 1986, p. 28.

2. M. Wendell Belew, "Introduction," in *Missions in the Mosaic,* comp. M. Wendell Belew (Atlanta: Home Mission Board of the Southern Baptist Convention, 1974), pp. 3-4.

3. C. Peter Wagner, "A Vision for Evangelizing the Real America," Plenary Session Address, National Convocation on Evangelizing Ethnic America, Houston, TX, 15 April 1985. (Printed.)

4. C. Peter Wagner, *Our Kind of People* (Atlanta: John Knox Press, 1979), pp. 38-40.

5. C. Kirk Hadaway, "The People of a New Ethnic America," in *Heirs of the Same Promise,* ed. Wesley D. Balda (Arcadia, CA: National Convocation on Evangelizing Ethnic America, 1984), pp. 41-43.

6. Fox Butterfield, "Why They Excell," *Parade Magazine,* 21 January 1990, p. 4.

7. Kenneth Eskey, "Hispanic Population Growing at Five Times

Rest of U.S.," *New Hampshire Sunday News,* 15 October 1989, sec. B, p. 8.

8. Michael Tutterow, "Southern Baptists Stress Language and Culture," *The Mandate,* October 1985, p. 8.

9. J.V. Thomas and David Arp, "How To Determine the Need for New Mission/Church Units," in *How to Start New Mission/Churches: A Guide for Associational Mission Leaders,* eds. J.V. Thomas and Carl A. Elder (Dallas: Baptist General Convention of Texas, 1979), p. 7.

THE CHALLENGE
OF THE ETHNIC MOSAIC

The American ethnic mosaic is composed of culturally identifiable people groups who have not been
completely assimilated into the dominant Anglo-American culture, but instead have retained their old world
ways. Although the United States has seen a mixing of
cultures, traditions, outlooks, and lifestyles over the
years and has experienced an overt standardization of
the country, especially in the area of the English language, uniqueness and individuality remain. Ethnic
diversity has not disappeared in America, despite pre-
dictions to the contrary.

This pluralistic society is comprised of a nation of
groups, each with its own set of needs, its own cultural
values, its own struggle for identity, and its own way of

hearing and appropriating the gospel of Christ. The challenging complexity of this nation's multi-cultural society must be addressed by the Anglo-American church.

THE COMPLEXITY OF THE ETHNIC MOSAIC

Ethnicity gives self-identity to the social sub-groups of the nation and determines what a person eats for breakfast, what he wears to a funeral, when he celebrates a holy day, whom he marries, and where he lives. Ethnicity is complex and has a powerful influence on human behavior and identity and also on the proclamation of the gospel.

Americans, including Christian churches, have not always considered the United States to be a pluralistic society of ethnic groups characterized by their heritage, culture, language, and lifestyle. The founding fathers of America adopted the motto, "*e pluribus unum* (one of many)," believing that ethnic diversity would give way to cultural homogeneity. This concept of blending together through the process of Americanization became known as the "melting pot."

The earliest commentators in American history emphasized this assimilation of the American people to an Anglo-uniformity. John Jay in *The Federalist* papers of 1787 spoke of "one united people, a people descended from the same ancestors, speaking the same language, professing the same religion, attached to the same principle of government, very similar in their manners and customs.[1]

This view of conforming to the dominant Anglo-Saxon culture continued into the Nineteenth Century in a less political yet more poetic figure when Ralph Waldo Emerson used the melting pot metaphor in his writings. This figure was further popularized in 1908 in a romantic and idealistic play by Israel Zangwill, entitled "The Melting Pot."[2] These generations who embraced the melting pot ideal made it difficult for many Americans to acknowledge the ethnic diversity and cultural pluralism which persisted in American society.

In the 1960's, however, it became apparent that the melting pot did not happen. The tension of the Civil Rights Movement forced most Americans to recognize that the ethnic groups in this nation had not "melted" and lost their cultural identity. Each group maintained ethnic differences and retained their unique characteristics so that the United States was seen as a mosaic, interwoven with a variety of cultures and experiences. The massive ethnic groups that made up the multi-ethnic fabric of American society were distinct in cultural traits, language, and religious practices from the dominant white, Anglo-Saxon, Protestant influence.[3]

Ethnic conformity to the Anglo-American standard did happen to some degree, especially among the ethnic groups which were closer to the cultural values and behavioral styles of Anglo-Saxon Protestant America. Many ethnics over the years had integrated into Anglo-American society, as the European immigrants of the last century did. Yet, many millions had wanted, without leaving their ethnic identity, to become Americans. These ethnic people remained "unmelted" either because they only planned on staying in America a short time or because they stayed isolated in their own cultural and language communities, creating no need to assimilate.

These ethnic groups brought to America their own distinctive styles of life, profoundly influencing the American population and uniquely enriching American society. St. Patrick's Day, Mexican restaurants, and Mardi Gras parades are evidence that much of the language, food, music, and other cultural characteristics which were once ethnic peculiarities are now part of the common American heritage. Ethnic groups have contributed their complementary parts to the whole of American society and have uniquely impacted the America's cultural landscape.

The impact of the ethnic presence in America is not simple, but rather is a complex phenomenon of differences and distinctions which are both predictable and surprising. For various reasons, multitudes of culturally identifiable ethnic groups in America have maintained their old world ways, native language, and customs. Moreover, they have remained nearly as isolated from the gospel preached in America as they were in their homelands. This means that the Anglo-American church must see beyond the American ideal of homogeneity, must face the ethnic differences in American society, and must develop a sensitivity to the challenge of diversity in culture, language, and religion which confronts it in the proclamation of the gospel to the rainbow of ethnic peoples in this country.

THE CHALLENGE OF CULTURE

Culture is the first significant challenge to the

evangelization of this multi-cultural society. In fact, because ethnic identity stems largely from an individual's affiliation with a given ethnic culture, cultural factors must be considered and used effectively in the proclamation of the gospel.[4]

Strong cultural ties are characterized by distinctive norms of conduct, beliefs, values, and skills which affect the subjectivity of individuals as well as their outward behavior. Culture actually shapes the way people talk, eat, think, interact with others, perceive values, and practice their faith. Christian outreach must consider these factors. Because Christian conversion takes place only in the context of ethnic culture, Anglo-American Christians must recognize cultural difference and must present the gospel in a way that can be culturally understood.

To meet this challenge of culture, the Anglo-American church first needs to learn to accept a variety of cultural origins as valid and needs to praise God for ethnic diversity. God as the Creator has made individuals different and has not limited the Christian faith to one cultural context. No culture holds a mandatory standard for all people or situations, and, thus, faith in Christ can be expressed in as many ways as there are cultures.

If the Anglo-American church neglects other ethnic cultures, it will be denying the reality of the diversity of God's creation and will be overlooking the cultural identity which is important to over half of this country's population. Learning to accept the complexity and subtlety of the nation's many different cultures will cultivate a sensitivity in the church to the varieties of

America's ethnic groups and will create a context for more effective evangelistic efforts.[5]

Secondly, if the Anglo-American church is to meet this evangelistic challenge, it needs to give up the notion that all ethnic groups of necessity must conform to the Anglo-American lifestyle to become Christians. This subtle pressure has often been placed on ethnic peoples, and as a result, the gospel has not been appealing to many from non-Anglo cultural groups.

The goal of the Anglo-American church should not be to erase ethnic culture, demand conformity to its Anglo-American lifestyle, or Americanize those in the ethnic communities. The church, instead, should concentrate on the goal of making disciples in the context of ethnic culture and should celebrate the positive contribution which ethnic diversity can make to the Kingdom of God.[6]

Thirdly, to meet the challenge of culture, the Anglo-American church needs to become creative in teaching and preaching the gospel within the culture of the other ethnic populations. Many well-meaning, but uninformed or insensitive, Anglo-American Christians have failed to reflect cultural sensitivity in their evangelistic proclamation and thus have alienated other ethnics from the gospel. Anglo-American Christians should develop an ability to apply the teachings of the Bible to the ethnic culture and should devise presentations of the gospel which are culturally sensitive and relevant.[7]

THE CHALLENGE OF LANGUAGE

Language is also a significant challenge to sharing

the gospel with the multitude of ethnic groups in America. Language is the primary means of communication, and since most of the multitudes of immigrants who arrive in America cannot speak English, language is one of the greatest barriers to the spread of the gospel. Many ethnic peoples cling to their native languages, making communication of God's Word by English-speakers virtually impossible.

To meet this challenge of language, the Anglo-American church first needs to recognize the tenacity of the language that draws non-Anglos together and needs to attempt to learn and communicate the gospel in the indigenous language of the ethnic group. In many cases, this will necessitate that the church raise up bilingual workers for cross cultural evangelism in the United States and train ethnics to evangelize their own people.[8]

Secondly, Anglo-American Christians need to abandon the attitude of insisting that all ethnics learn English in order to live in America and to hear the gospel message. This approach of assuming that everyone must know English has caused many ethnic peoples to lose any opportunity of being saved. In order to reach them with the gospel, the Anglo-American church must communicate its message in the language of the people.[9]

Thirdly, the Anglo church in America needs to realize that communicating the gospel requires more than a knowledge of another language. Effective communication necessitates an awareness of the non-verbal and cultural aspects conveyed through facial expression, gestures, and tone of voice. Just because a Christian knows another language does not mean that he understands the complexities of communication in that language. Care must be taken to consider all of the factors in communication, so that the message conveyed is what is intended.[10]

THE CHALLENGE OF RELIGION

Religion, likewise, is a significant challenge to the evangelization of this multi-cultural nation. The religious culture of a people is often intertwined with their ethnic identity. In fact, to many ethnic peoples in America, religious affiliation has become more significant than national origin or cultural heritage. In the perception of many, religion provides meaning and social connectedness.[11] As a result, groups such as Armenian Orthodox, Chinese Buddhist, French Catholics, Pakistani Muslims, and Utah Mormons, find their sense of belonging and identity in their religion.

Although the importance of religious identity may vary from situation to situation and from group to group, many ethnic groups possess their own distinctive religious character. For them, religion is not so much personal, as communal, and it influences every area of life. Among these ethnic groups, religious distinctiveness, such as the Italian "festa" for a patron saint, the Jewish "bar mitzvah," the Irish wake, and the peyotism of American Indians, has flourished as a part of ethnic behavior in America.[12]

The estimate of many statisticians is that nearly fifteen million adherents of non-Christian world religions reside in the United States today. Jews are the largest non-Christian group in America, numbering over five million. Nevertheless, by the year 2015, Islam with over four million American adherents in the early nineties will replace Judaism as the second largest religion in the United States, after Christianity.[13] Two million Hindus, four million Buddhists, 150,000 Sikhs, and many others who dwell in America maintain a religion that is a basic characteristic of their ethnic identity.[14]

Even though these ethnic groups consider themselves to be very religious, they need to hear the gospel and know the truth about salvation in Jesus Christ. Because of the religious pluralism among ethnic groups, Anglo-American Christians will be confronted with the perplexing problems and the cultural complexities of devout followers of other religious traditions as they attempt to communicate the Christian faith.[15]

To meet this evangelistic challenge which world religions bring to the Anglo-American church, Christians must recognize that the religious identity of many ethnic groups is not essentially different from their cultural and linguistic identity. Historical origins, cultural meaning, and religious emblems will need to be carefully understood by the church. Moreover, the gospel will need to be wisely and demonstratively presented in order to withstand the pressures of a dominant and complex religious culture. As Anglo-American Christians understand more about how religion relates to ethnic identity, new insights may be gained which will enable the church to more effectively evangelize in ethnic America.

The long cherished belief that ethnic pluralism in America can be denied, or at best overlooked, must be rooted out of the Anglo-American church if it is to meet the evangelistic challenge of the ethnic mosaic in this country. Becoming American has not meant dissolving all differences, losing identity, and melting into the general masses of the Anglo-American population. Cultural traits, language, and religious practices have been a part of the baggage with which ethnic people have arrived in this country, and they have contributed to the multi-colored, multi-lingual, and multi-cultural fabric of America.

This diversity and complexity of culture, language, and religion confronts the church in this country with an extraordinarily challenging evangelistic task. An effective proclamation of the gospel in America will involve considerably more attention to the ethnic pluralism of the United States than has been given by Anglo-American Christians.

Anglo-American Christians, of necessity, will need an increasingly greater awareness of the challenge of culture, language, and religion as they launch evangelistic programs. They will have to be creative in teaching the truths of Scripture within the cultural, linguistic, and religious context. A heightened understanding of the challenging complexities of ethnicity in America should provide insights which will enable the Anglo-American church to reap a greater harvest in ethnic America and thus impact the ethnic peoples of the world for Christ.

Endnotes

1. John Jay, *The Federalist*, 1787, quoted in Harold J. Abramson, "Assimilation and Pluralism," in *Harvard Encyclopedia of American Ethnic Groups*, ed. Stephen Thernstrom (Cambridge, MA: Harvard University Press, 1980), p. 152.

2. Harold J. Abramson, "Assimilation and Pluralism," in *Harvard Encyclopedia of American Ethnic Groups*, ed. Stephen Thernstrom (Cambridge, MA: Harvard University Press, 1980), pp. 152-153.

3. Wagner, *Our Kind*, pp. 8, 45-51.

4. James N. Lewis, *Ministry/Witness Resource Guide: Internationals* (Atlanta: Home Mission Board of the Southern Baptist Convention, 1987), pp. 8-10.

5. Ibid.

6. Tetsunao Yamamori, *"God's New Envoys"* (Portland, OR: Multnomah Press, 1987), p. 152.

7. Oscar Romo, "Ministering with Hispanic Americans," in *Missions in the Mosaic*, pp. 45-47.

8. Earl Parvin, *MissionsUSA* (Chicago: Moody Press, 1985), p. 42.

9. Alex D. Montoya, *Hispanic Ministry in North America* (Grand Rapids, MI: Zondervan Publishing House, 1987), p. 11.

10. Lewis, *Internationals*, pp. 8-10

11. Wagner, *Our Kind*, pp. 64-65.

12. Harold J. Abramson, "Religion," in *Harvard Encyclopedia of American Ethnic Groups*, ed. Stephen Thernstrom (Cambridge, MA: Harvard University Press, 1980), pp. 869, 870, 872.

13. Don Tingle, "Over Here," *Asian Evangelism*, October-December 1987, p. 3.

14. Parvin, *MissionsUSA*, pp. 168-179.

15. Harold Netland, "Evangelical Theology of Mission and the Challenge of Pluralism," *Trinity World Forum*, Fall 1989, p. 1.

THE DIVERSITY
OF THE ETHNIC MOSAIC

Individuals from around the globe, speaking every language and representing every nationality, race, and religion, are arriving on America's shores each year. Some are trading the cool greenery of Northern European cities for the smog of Los Angeles and New York, while others are leaving the sweet smells of Southeast Asia for the pungent odor of exhaust fumes. Others still are crossing the South China Sea in small boats or are braving the Caribbean Sea in rafts made of inner tubes. Millions from throughout the world are added annually to the ethnic population of the nation.

This diverse population of ethnic peoples is transforming American cities, working in its factories, and changing its schools. This ethnic diversity has become a permanent part of the national fabric, yet many Americans do not realize that immigration is the most significant factor in the country's population growth. At least fifty million foreigners are projected to enter the United States during the next century, with millions more visiting for short periods of time.

Immigrants, refugees, migrants, international students, and other internationals, such as professionals, diplomats, tourists, and seamen, contribute to the wide diversity of people who are taking up permanent and temporary residence in this ethnic mosaic. Many of these people are arriving from cultural groups which restrict missionary activity or from countries whose doors are closed to traditional missionaries. This influx of new ethnic groups provides the Anglo-American church with a unique opportunity for mission ministry within America's borders and gives the majority of Anglo-Christians the opportunity to have an impact in the evangelization of the world by reaching peoples from the world in their own backyard.

IMMIGRANTS

Immigrants are individuals who come to America to establish permanent residence and possible citizenship. Since the Immigration Act of 1965 repealed the national quotas, a dramatic increase has occurred in the number of new immigrants. During the eighties alone the legal immigration to the United States was more than one million persons per year, with perhaps two million more entering illegally each year. As a result, not since the first decade of the Twentieth Century have so many immigrants acquired American citizenship.

These new immigrants have included persons of all races, cultures, linguistic abilities, and creeds, with particularly large influxes of Asians and Latin Americans. Most of them have come to get a job so that they can support their families. In most cases they have been eager and dependable workers, accepting unattractive, low-paying jobs that most Americans reject. With them they have brought to America a willingness to take a risk, a readiness to work hard, a desire to master English, a reluctance to depend on government aid, and a need for salvation in Jesus Christ.

Although many immigrants bring strong religious beliefs with them to America, the first generation newcomers often are more open to the gospel than other segments of the American population. However, many of them have adapted quickly to the materialism and secularism of American culture, leaving little room for the gospel. After ten to fifteen years in the United States, these people have little interest in hearing the good news of Jesus. Anglo-American Christians need to concentrate evangelistic efforts on new immigrants while they are most open and receptive.

REFUGEES

Refugees are people who, because of persecution, oppression, or calamity, have left their homelands and are unable or unwilling to return. The journey for many has been difficult and extremely dangerous. Many have fled the nightmare of Cambodia, have escaped the attacks of ruthless Thai pirates, have endured long months in crowded refugee camps, or have crossed the dangerous waters of the Caribbean. Having struggled with persecution and with separation from family, friends, and homeland, they have come to America to find the peace and acceptance they have never known.

Even though refugees make up only about five percent of the total immigration into this country, more than a million from throughout the world have relocated in the United States in the past decade, with tens of thousands still entering annually. Most of these refugees have, contrary to expectation, bolstered the economy by accepting jobs that few others wanted and by becoming remarkably self-sufficient.[1] They have been eager, hardworking, and honest people who desired quickly to become self-supporting.

Upon arriving in America, most refugees have been highly responsive to the gospel. Because their lives have been shattered by brutality and betrayal, refugees are searching for meaning in life. They are open to God's love among Christians and to the hope which the gospel can offer. In many instances Christians have fed them in refugee camps overseas, Christians have met them at the airport, and Christians have helped them adjust to American life. Since religious groups have settled over three-fourths of the refugees who have entered the United States in the past fifteen years, it is not surprising that many refugees have responded to the gospel.[2]

For the Anglo-American church, the thousands of refugees who have sought asylum in this country over the past few years are a mission opportunity at its doorstep. Hundreds of thousands of people remain in refugee camps around the world or in relocation centers in the United States, waiting for a sponsor who can settle them permanently in this peaceful land. The Anglo-American church must resist turning the task of refugee resettlement over to relief agencies or cultic groups.

Moreover, some refugees encounter isolation after several months in the United States, feel lost and rejected, and long to return to their homelands. Many others adapt to the American culture within two years of their arrival and have little room left for the gospel because they have returned half-heartedly to their traditional religion or have embraced the materialism and secularism of the West.[3] As refugees continue to contribute to the different cultures and ethnic backgrounds in the United States, the Anglo-American church needs to grasp the spiritual opportunities among refugees, demonstrate a genuine love and friendship to the newly arriving refugees in this country, and share the gospel with them while they are most open.

MIGRANT WORKERS

Two to four million migrant workers dwell in America, residing in most every state. They work in hotels and restaurants as bellboys, dishwashers, and busboys and in hospitals as orderlies and service staff. At harvest time, many agricultural areas of America depend on migrant workers to provide much of the hard labor in the fields, packing houses, and canneries. Migrating with the ripening harvests, they can be found in most areas of the United States during the summer and in Florida, Texas, and California the year-round.[4]

Many migrant workers come to America to stay for a season or a few years in order to save money and then to return to their homeland for a chance at a better life. Others come with a thought of going home, yet never do and are caught in the vicious cycle of poverty, unemployment, poor health, and inadequate education.

Migrant workers are generally youthful, poor, unskilled, and uneducated. They are often sick, and a large number speak a language other than English. A source of cheap labor, they are frequently recruited by labor contractors and exploited. Along with their families, they live at the bottom of the socio-economic ladder, working under conditions intolerable to other Americans. Moving from place to place with the seasonal needs of different crops, they may be white Appalachian, African American, Indian, Oriental, Canadian, Mexican, Puerto Rican, Haitian, or Jamaican.[5]

Plagued by divorce, separation, common-law marriages, and unwed parenthood, migrant workers need to be reached with the gospel. The mobility of migrants, their health, educational, and social needs, and the frequent language barrier make evangelization difficult and challenging.

Anglo-American Christians need to go with compassion and love to the worker camps where migrant families reside. They need to stand by migrants who are victims of injustice, cruelty, and prejudice and to supply relief in the times of pain and suffering, as they minister the gospel message in their midst.

INTERNATIONAL STUDENTS

Temporarily uprooted from familiar social, economic, cultural, and religious surroundings, nearly one-half million international students have come from over one hundred and eighty countries of the world to the colleges and universities of America. These international students have left behind everything that makes their life secure in order to succeed in achieving academic goals.

Most of these international students are preparing for leadership positions in their home countries. They will be appointed in the next twenty-five years to one-fourth to one-half of the top political, military, economic, scientific, and academic positions in the world.[6] International students in the United States today are the world leaders of the Twenty-first Century.

The majority of these students have never heard the gospel, and nearly half are from countries where traditional mission work is restricted or outlawed. However, most international students speak English, and many want to know about the Christian faith. Others will accept a Bible and read it.

Often lonely and sometimes depressed, they are eager for an American to talk with them and to befriend them. As a result, many are delighted to visit a Christian home and are willing to spend hours discussing the scriptures with a Christian who takes a sincere and personal interest in them.[7]

Fig. 2. International Student Population

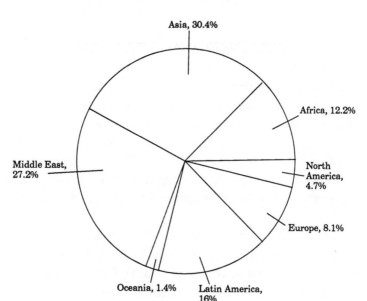

By reaching international students from countries closed to the gospel, Christian churches in America could impact the world for Christ. Students who become Christians in America can return to their homes as dedicated servants of God, where they can share the gospel and plant churches. Language and culture are not barriers to them, and even closed doors cannot keep them out. The potential for evangelizing the world through international students is tremendous.

Lamentably, however, most international students will return home without an American friend and without hearing the gospel. Eighty percent of the international students in this country never have an

American friend,[8] and it is estimated that less than one-fourth of one percent of them are being reached through the witness of Anglo-American Christians.[9] Many thousands are returning to their homelands and may never again have the opportunity to hear the gospel.

The presence of foreign students on American campuses offers Anglo-American Christians unique opportunities for cross-cultural evangelism without visas, restrictions, or language barriers. The time has come for Anglo-American Christians to reach across the cultural barriers to these international students, to provide God-centered hospitality to students in their Christian homes, and to show active Christian concern and loving friendship to the tens of thousands of international students on this nation's college and university campuses.

INTERNATIONAL PROFESSIONALS, DIPLOMATS, TOURISTS, AND SEAMEN

Millions of international professionals, diplomats, tourists, and seamen annually visit and live in the United States on a temporary visa. They are in the United States for a limited period of time and become residents for a few days or several years. The Iraqi doctor, the Japanese tourist, the Saudi oilman, the Peruvian seaman, and the Soviet diplomat come from scattered corners of the world.

Some face financial crises and job insecurity, while others function as the most influential and well-educated members of their nation's society. They represent a diverse community that is here today and gone tomorrow, yet is daily replaced by a growing influx of non-immigrant visitors who work, study, and sight-see in the United States.[10]

Fig. 3. Internationals in the United States

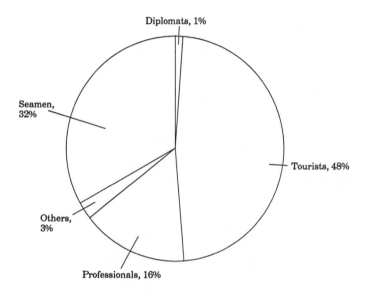

This group of internationals is proving to be one of the great untapped mission fields in the world. Many of these visitors are from nations where Christianity is a minority religion. Some have never met a Christian. Because of Lebanon or Ireland, others see Christianity merely as a political, not spiritual, movement. Outside their own environments, however, many of these internationals are more likely to listen to the Christian message in the United States than in their homelands.[11]

Contacts made and friendships built with Anglo-

American Christians can ignite interest in the gospel and can translate into changed lives and a new faith. The more than sixty nations which are presently closed to missionary endeavors and the many other countries which prohibit or limit the outreach of the church could be transformed by the influence of returning countrymen whose lives have been touched by the power of God in America.[12]

Over ninety percent of the earth's nations are represented by tourists, in businesses, by seamen, and through diplomatic embassies in the United States. These internationals may be found in educational centers, medical complexes, governmental institutions, trade centers, seaports, and almost every village, town, or city across the country. Through contacts made and friendships built, Christians can ignite an interest in the gospel among them and can utilize opportunities for evangelizing the world through them.[13]

Developing friendships in this transient non-immigrant community, however, will not be easy. Many internationals maintain cultural, linguistic, and political idiosyncrasies which may create barriers for the proclamation of the gospel. As a result, the Anglo-American church's witness will need to be life-style in nature. It will necessitate nurturing friendship and respect and will require cultural sensitivity. Anglo-American Christians need to learn to witness and minister to internationals who are more open to the gospel in America than in their home nations and who have the potential for a global influence for the cause of Christ.

Certainly the diversity in the ethnic mosaic of America is enormous, with peoples of every hue and from every shore coming to America. Immigrants, refugees, migrant workers, foreign students, and internationals reside in this nation's communities. At the end of the Twentieth Century cross-cultural mission frontiers are no longer only in China, the Middle East, Asia, South America, and Africa. They can be found in Miami, New York, Houston, Chicago, and Los Angeles in the presence of ethnic people from around the world.

Anglo Christians in the United States can actually impact the world for Christ through these indigenous ethnic peoples from virtually every country of the world. No visas, no government restrictions, and total religious freedom in America make it possible to spread the gospel to this mixture of ethnic groups and to tap this pool of potential missionaries. The possibilities for global evangelism are limitless. Anglo-American churches merely need to reach the mission field that waits in the migrant worker camps, relocation centers, seaports, dorms, apartments, and condos of their communities.

Endnotes

1. Beth Spring, "Refugees: Off Sinking Boats Into American Churches," *Christianity Today*, 15 June 1984, p. 29.

2. Alec Hill, "Ministry Among Newcomers," in *Heirs of the Same Promise*, ed. Wesley D. Balda (Arcadia, CA: National Convocation on Evangelizing Ethnic America, 1984), pp. 79-81.

3. Michael Tutterow, "More Evangelical Attention Needed For 'Newcomers'," *The Mandate*, October 1985, p. 5.

4. Cecil D. Etheredge, *Ministry/Witness Resource Guide: Migrants* (Atlanta, GA: Home Mission Board of the Southern Baptist Convention, 1985), pp. 4-6.

5. Parvin, *MissionsUSA*, pp. 113-119.

6. Lawson Lau, *The World At Your Doorstep* (Downers Grove, IL: InterVarsity Press, 1984), p. 13.

7. *An American Friend Handbook* (Colorado Springs, CO: International Students Incorporated, 1984), p. 1.

8. Roy Weece, "Jesus Voted Yes!", *Christian Standard*, 26 July 1987, pp. 4-5.

9. Lau, *The World At Your Doorstep*, p. 13.

10. See Oscar Romo, "Twentieth-Century Sojourners," *MissionsUSA*, January-February 1987, p. 33, and Kristin Kvaalen, "Seamen's Mission: Gateway to the Unreached Peoples," *Mission Frontiers*, June-July 1989, pp. 4-7.

11. Everett Hullum, "The Internationals: The Diplomats," *MissionsUSA*, May-June 1987, pp. 12, 17.

12. Joe Westbury, "The Internationals: The Tourists," *MissionsUSA*, September-October 1987, pp. 9-14.

13. Lewis, *Internationals*, pp. 4-7.

THE MAKE-UP
OF THE ETHNIC MOSAIC

Over two hundred language and people groups, plus over three hundred American Indian tribes, now reside in America, swelling the ethnic population in excess of one hundred million. Some ethnics have established themselves in this country, while new arrivals are entering the United States daily. The make-up of the ethnic mosaic is constantly changing and is profoundly affecting America.

Many of these ethnic peoples who make up this multi-cultural nation have been an invisible presence in American society for decades. Domestic workers in Southern California, business owners in New York City, clerks in Florida, dress makers in Chicago, and farm laborers in Michigan have been present on the American landscape, yet not seen. But now non-Anglo Americans are also doctors, company executives, politicians, and television personalities. They are touching every aspect of this multi-cultural society and are leaving their impact.

City supermarkets now carry an extraordinary variety of ethnic foods and goods. Book stores do a thriving business in practical language manuals. Manufacturing companies employ workers who speak a plurality of languages. Urban high schools have a distinctly ethnic look, with many ethnic students excelling academically. The mixture of ethnic groups now appears in every area of American life with such complex intermingling that a fast food stand in Hollywood which is operated by Koreans sells kosher tacos and the best Thai restaurant in Houston has a Mexican cook.

Tens of millions from distinct people groups, who have forsaken the land of their ancestors to come to America, constitute this perplexing, yet remarkable, ethnic mosaic. They are the Anglo-American church's great, forgotten, mission field. Several of the major ethnic groupings comprising America's ethnic make-up and needing to be evangelized are Hispanics, Asians, Europeans, American Indians, Africans and Caribbeans and Middle Easterners.

HISPANICS

The Spanish-speaking population of multi-cultural America will soon be this nation's largest minority. By the early 1990's the number of Hispanics in the United

States had surpassed twenty million, with another six to eight million illegals, and their number was growing at five times the rate of the rest of the population.[1]

Millions of Hispanics are continuing to come across the Rio Grande from Mexico, up from Central and South America, and over the Caribbean from Puerto Rico and Cuba. The largest number of immigrants settle in California, Texas, and New York, with significant Hispanic populations also in Florida, Arizona, Colorado, New Mexico, Illinois and New Jersey.

As a result of this Latinization of America, the United States is now the fourth largest Spanish-speaking nation in the world. Spanish is now commonly heard in America's big cities. In south Florida, businesses hang out signs "English spoken here." In New York City, bus and subway billboards for familiar products are increasingly found in Spanish. In California, special yellow pages in Spanish have been published by the telephone company. In Texas, Spanish is the language of the border counties. Even though over fifty percent of Hispanics in America are bilingual, loyalty to the Spanish language persists and will continue.

Although the Spanish language and culture are shared by all Hispanics, they are a mixture of several distinctive subcultural groups with a variety of peoples and customs. Mexicans are most numerous, followed by Puerto Ricans, Cubans, and other Latin Americans. To the untrained eyes, they may all seem to be the same, but for anyone who wishes to share the gospel among Hispanics it is essential to recognize that they are a diverse group of all these nationalities who are not all alike in background and history. They are a heterogeneous population comprised of two dozen ethnic groups and representing a tremendous cross-section of the Spanish-speaking world.[2]

Fig. 4. Type of Hispanic Population

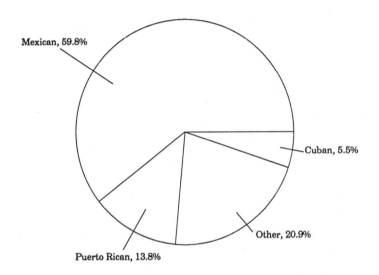

Hispanics have a rich heritage where family loyalty, dignity of the individual, hospitality, and a joy of living are valued. Nevertheless, these are being destroyed by the materialism of America, and this deep heritage is losing ground in the lives of Hispanics.

Tradition, including religious tradition, no longer plays as important of a role. Fewer than twenty percent actively cling to Catholicism, five percent are Protestants, and the remainder attend no church. While the church in Latin America experiences unprecedented growth, Hispanics in the United States are largely unevangelized.[3] These Spanish-speakers present a tremendous evangelistic challenge to the Anglo-American church.

ASIANS

Asians, along with Hispanics, comprise eighty percent of the legal immigration to the United States and are the fastest growing segment of America's non-Anglo population. They have increased by over five hundred percent in the past twenty-five years. Two out of five immigrants in this country are now Asian, and Asians are projected to total nearly ten million in population by the turn of the century.[4]

For more than one hundred years immigrants have come to the United States from Asia, beginning with the Chinese and Japanese. Though traditionally assumed to be the largest Asian groups, Chinese and Japanese are surpassed by Filipinos, who represent the largest number of Asians in this multi-cultural society. More recently, people from India, Korea, and Southeast Asia have flooded America's shores in growing numbers.[5]

Most Asian immigrants are peoples whose background originates in the part of Asia which is south and east of the Himalayas. Nevertheless, although these Asians come from the same geographic area of the world, numerous varieties of cultural traditions exist among them, including differences in history, religion, language, culture, and values.

The Chinese whose ancestors came to the West Coast

soon after the discovery of gold has little in common with the Cambodian fisherman. The educated, highly motivated Korean has no sense of identity with the Vietnamese refugee. The young, professional Asian Indian has little similarity with the Filipino laborer. Each Asian group has its own unique characteristics, languages, and cultures.

Fig. 5. Type of Asian Population

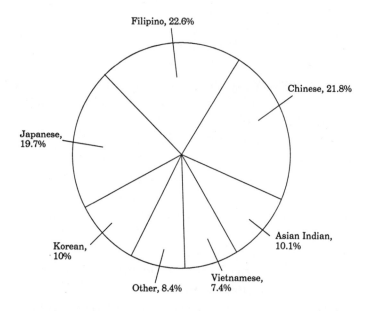

Typically Asian immigrants are nominally Buddhist, Hindu, or animist. Many have never heard of Christianity, and most have never met a Christian. Some estimates indicate that less than six percent of Asians in America are being reached by the Anglo-American church, although many Koreans have been evangelized through the Christian workers sent by strong Korean churches and some Southeast Asian refugees have embraced Christianity after witnessing the love of their Christian sponsors.[6]

The Anglo-American church needs to intensify its efforts to meet the challenge of evangelizing the diverse Asian population which makes up the ethnic mosaic. Anglo-American Christians need to minister to the overseas-born Asians who speak a variety of languages and dialects and maintain their cultural heritage. At the same time, they need to reach out to the American-born Asians who speak English, have adopted many of the American styles, ideas, and values, and yet retain much of the ethnic identity and cultural character of their parents.

EUROPEANS

Even though the percentage of all immigrants has shifted to peoples from Latin American and Asian cultures, America has historically received large numbers of immigrants from Europe. Europeans constitute more than one-fourth of the nation's total population and have contributed much to the ethnic diversity of America.[7]

European immigrants have come from thirty-four continental countries, making Europeans a linguistic and cultural mixture of subcultures in America. The Germanic peoples, which include immigrants from Germany, Austria, and Switzerland, form the largest European ethnic group. Settling in the urban centers of the Northeast and on the farms of the Midwest, peoples of German ancestry have preserved their language and culture through their Lutheran and Roman Catholic churches and schools.

The Scandinavians, from Sweden, Denmark, Norway, and Iceland, and the British, from England, Ireland, and Scotland, comprise the next two largest European ethnic groups and have been the groups to absorb most easily into the Anglo-American culture. Iron curtain countries, including Poland and Czechoslovakia, make up the Baltic and Slavic European groups, and they contribute a most interesting and colorful cultural heritage to America's multi-ethnic society.

The Latins, among whom are French, Italians, Portuguese, and Romanians, have taken jobs in the industrial centers of the North, have maintained strong family ties, and have enriched the American diet with their zesty cuisine. Other European ethnics, including Greeks and European Jews, round out the groups who once immigrated to the United States in the millions annually.[8]

The religious background of European ethnics is largely Lutheran and Roman Catholic. For some, their religious faith is still vibrant and active, but for most, their religion is nominal and seldom practiced. Evangelistic outreach to European groups will need to seek contacts with immigrants caught in the cultural, linguistic, and religious transformation of passing into the American mainstream and will require sharing the gospel in all its excitement and relevancy.

AMERICAN INDIANS

Native Americans, who reside as citizens of sovereign nations within the boundaries of the United States, contribute to the assortment of ethnic peoples in America. American Indians, Eskimos, and Aleuts represent over three hundred tribes and Amerindian dialects and are as numerous today as when Columbus landed in the New World.[9]

All fifty states contain Indian populations, yet eighty percent live west of the Mississippi River. Because of the need to locate jobs, however, Native Americans are becoming more numerous in the cities of America than on the reservation. Urban centers, such as Los Angeles and New York, have tens of thousands of Indians hidden away in their central cities.[10]

Contrary to popular thought, neither reservation nor urban Indian populations are culturally close, but rather maintain great tribal diversity. Similarities, however, exist with native religions, though various tribes have religious peculiarities. The Native American Church, or peyotism, syncretistically combines the Aztec and the Christian religion and has a wide appeal to large groups of American Indians.[11]

With less than five percent of American Indians estimated to be Christians, this segment of the ethnic population needs to receive the evangelistic attention of the church through culturally relevant presentations of the message of the gospel. Evangelization, however, will be challenging. Because of historical mistreatment, Indians will not easily accept the gospel message from the lips of white men. The training of Native Americans to reach their own people, therefore, will be a vital key to their evangelization. Moreover, the isolation of urban Indians from tight Indian communities will make outreach and church planting difficult among the forty-five percent who dwell in American cities.

AFRICANS AND CARIBBEANS

Millions of people who dwell in America are of African descent, numbering about twelve percent of the population. The descendants of the emancipated slaves are the largest African group; nevertheless, they retain a heritage which is more Anglo than African.[12] Because these black Americans have unique needs which must be considered for reaching them with the gospel, the state of black evangelism in the United States needs to be carefully examined by the Anglo church.

Those African ethnic groups, however, whose primary language and culture identity is other than English include the over one million immigrants from Subsaharan Africa, new-comers from the Caribbean islands, and foreign students on America's college and university campuses.[13] These African and Caribbean peoples have an ethnic heritage that is distinguished from any Anglo orientation, and evangelization of these groups will require crossing cultural barriers to reach them with the gospel.

Blacks, Africans, and Caribbeans in America are largely urban, yet are located in nearly every major American community. Large numbers of African-Americans have migrated to the urban centers of the United States, contributing to a black majority population in such cities as Detroit, Atlanta, and Washington, D.C. At the same time, tens of thousands of African international students study on American campuses, and millions of Caribbean Islanders are peopling the major metropolitan areas along the eastern coastline of North America.

The spiritual plight of Blacks in America has long been overlooked by Anglo-American Christians. The "whiteness" of many American churches is evidence of this neglect. While some estimates indicate that nearly fifty percent of the African-American, African, and Caribbean populations in the United States are unchurched. Moreover, many African-Americans are listening to the Muslim missionaries from Africa who are working in the black communities, and they are turning to Islam in their desperate search for answers to their spiritual needs. With only four countries in Africa having a greater population than the non-Christian Blacks in the United States, a tremendous mission opportunity exists among African-Americans, Africans, and Caribbeans who live in this nation.[14]

As other ethnic groups, many African and Caribbean ethnics hold cultural ideals and values which they cherish, and they maintain a strong affection for their homeland. Awareness of these ethnic differences and preferences will be necessary as the Anglo church ministers the gospel among Haitians, Ethiopians, Jamaicans, Nigerians, and others of African background who have come to America. Moreover, Anglo Christians will need to acknowledge that many African-Americans will feel more comfortable in churches and Bible study groups where the music, styles of worship, and church programs are meaningful to the black culture.

MIDDLE EASTERNERS

Living among American's potpourri of ethnic peoples are nearly three million Middle Easterners, including Saudi Arabians, Turks, Lebanonese, Jordanians, Iranians, Egyptians, Syrians, and Iraqis. Ninety percent of these Middle Easterners settle in cities, and half of this population can be found in the seven states of Illinois, Ohio, Michigan, Massachusetts, Georgia, Texas, and California.[15]

The varied backgrounds and the stress Middle Easterners place on their differences encourages immigrants in America to gather in separate, close-knit communities where the sub-cultures retain their culture, religion, and social life.[16] Strong religious heritage, fierce national pride, and tenacious family and linguistic loyalty allow Middle Easterners to maintain their unique identities and cultures in this country.

The majority of Middle Easterners are Muslim, contributing to the rapid growth of Islam in the United States. Though some are nominal in their belief, many are pressing hard to evangelize Americans into the Muslim community. The over six hundred mosques and Islamic teaching centers in the United States are evidence of the profound religious influence that Muslims and Middle Easterners are having in America.[17] Even though Middle Easterners are largely Muslim in their faith, it also should be remembered that ten percent of this population are Christians and thousands are Jews.

Christian witness among Middle Easterners and awareness by Anglo-American churches of the presence of Middle Easterners in their communities is urgent and necessary. Anglo-American Christians need to learn how to reach those who follow the teachings of Islam, without isolating them from family or cultural background, and to organize efforts to present the gospel to them.

The rainbow of colors, languages, and cultural traditions in the ethnic groupings which make up America's ethnic mosaic present the church in this country with a tremendous opportunity and an awesome responsibility for cross-cultural evangelism. Anglo-American Christians need to work diligently to reach Hispanics, Asians, Europeans, American Indians, Africans and Caribbeans, Middle Easterners, and other non-Anglo ethnics with the gospel. America's great, forgotten, mission field is ripe for harvest among these millions of distinct cultural and linguistic groups which are a part of this multi-cultural, multi-ethnic nation.

Endnotes

1. See Randolph E. Schmid, "U.S. Hispanic Population Continues Growth," *New Hampshire Sunday News*, 18 March 1990, sec. B, p. 4, and Eskey, "Hispanic Population Growing," p. 8.

2. Parvin, *MissionsUSA*, p. 108.

3. Ibid., pp. 122-124.

4. Butterfield, "Why They Excel," p. 4.

5. Oscar Romo, "The Asian Challenge," *MissionsUSA*, January-February 1990, p. 44.

6. Parvin, *MissionsUSA*, pp. 131, 144.

7. Home Mission Board of the Southern Baptist Convention, Language Missions Division, *We're Working With Europeans Through Language Missions*, Atlanta, GA, 1986. (Pamphlet.)

8. Walker L. Knight, "Ministering With European Language Groups," in *Missions In The Mosaic*, comp. M. Wendell Belew (Atlanta, GA: Home Missions Board of the Southern Baptist Convention, 1974), pp. 59-63.

9. Home Mission Board of the Southern Baptist Convention, *Language Missions Facts: 1988 Update*, Atlanta, GA, 1988. (Pamphlet.)

10. Parvin, *MissionsUSA*, pp. 55, 58, 68.

11. Frank Belvin, "Ministering With American Indians," in *Missions in the Mosaic*, comp. M. Wendell Belew (Atlanta, GA: Home Mission Board of the Southern Baptist Convention, 1974), pp. 12-16.

12. The scope of this book is limited to those ethnic groups whose primary language and culture identity is other than English. As a result, although greater attention needs to be given by the Anglo church to the evangelization of blacks in United States, this work will not discuss in detail the importance and need for focusing on outreach to black Americans.

13. See *Language Missions Facts*, p. 2 and Parvin, *MissionsUSA*, p. 101.

14. Parvin, *MissionsUSA*, pp. 75, 77.

15. Home Mission Board of the Southern Baptist Convention, *We're Working With Middle Easterners Through Language Missions*, Atlanta, GA, 1986. (Pamphlet.)

16. International Missions, "Eastern Religions in North America," Wayne, NJ: n.d. (Mimeographed.)

17. Tingle, "Over Here," p. 3.

THE STATE
OF THE ETHNIC MOSAIC

Uprooted from home and homeland, millions of ethnic immigrants have come to America seeking a better life. Some have fled the nightmare of political oppression, others have escaped the hardship of an impoverished existence, while still others have sought the business possibilities in this land of economic opportunity. Limited by language, employment, education, and social customs, many have faced the shock of adjusting to their new environment and the alienation of settling in this new country.

The traumas, difficulties, and needs facing the peoples in the ethnic mosaic have been affected by the geographic location, the social situation, and the spiritual condition of the various ethnic groups. The state of the ethnics in the United States provide the Anglo-American church with a great missions challenge.

GEOGRAPHIC LOCATION

Ethnic peoples can be found in nearly every community across the fifty states, but concentrations of different ethnic groups are located in several places. When America was first being settled by immigrants, they came to New England, the Carolinas, and what are now the mid-Atlantic states. Then, they headed west across the Appalachians. But, today California, Texas, and New York receive over sixty percent of America's newcomers,[1] and urban areas absorb as much as ninety percent of Hispanic and Asian immigrants.[2]

Various factors draw new arrivals to the geographic locations where they choose to settle or work. Some ethnics, like the Afghan refugees who have settled in Denver, Colorado, move to areas of the country where the geography and climate are most like their native homeland. Others, like the Hispanics of Mexican origin of whom eighty percent have their home in a band running parallel to the border with Mexico, tend to concentrate in the locations surrounding the natural points of entry. Still others, like the Middle Easterners who live in large Muslim communities in metropolitan Detroit, are attracted to the neighborhoods which contain family, friends, and fellow countrymen who immigrated to America at an earlier date.

International students go to the colleges and universities across the land, with huge numbers being attracted to several large schools in states such as California, Illinois, Ohio, and Pennsylvania which enroll tens of thousands of international students each year. Embassies and diplomatic missions in New York City and Washington, D.C. become home for two-thirds of the foreign diplomats who enter the United States each year, with scattered consulates and trade missions in major American cities drawing the remainder of the foreign personnel.

Tourists visit primarily the East and West coasts, while international seamen call in all of the major American port cities. Migrant workers follow the seasonal crops throughout the United States annually, moving as far north as New York, Michigan, and Minnesota in the summer and retreating to the homebase regions of California, Florida, and south Texas in the winter.

Sixty percent of the Asian ethnics live west of the Mississippi River. The majority of immigrants of Jewish ancestry reside in the Northeastern United States. South Florida is a favored destination of Latin American Hispanics, while New York City draws thousands of Puerto Ricans. California, the most populous state, attracts the largest number of ethnic immigrants, with nearly thirty percent of the new arrivals settling there.[3]

The geographic distribution of the non-Anglo population creates unique social situations among the various ethnic groups and presents the Anglo church with special challenges. Many ethnics in urban areas or among migrating peoples are outside the reach of traditional church programs which usually have not targeted these often "hidden" segments of the community. Careful attention needs to be given by the church to recognizing these populations and to developing relationships with them so that the gospel may be presented in a way that touches the hearts and lives of those in these mixtures of ethnic groups which are geographically spread across the nation.

SOCIAL SITUATION

Although all ethnics are not deprived economically or educationally, many arrive in this country with no money, no family, and no place to live. Frequently, these immigrants have been forced to leave their countries because of ever increasing political, social, and economic turmoil and have come to America from desperate and deprived conditions in their homelands.

Leaving what few belongings they have and severing ties with family and friends, they are faced with the shock of separation from the familiar. Their arrival creates physical, emotional, economic, housing, educational, and employment problems for them and their family. Eager to begin their new life in this land of opportunity, they take whatever jobs are available, often working long hours for meager wages.

Some immigrants from Asia and elsewhere are professionals and from the upper class, but many other immigrants have a limited education and are poor. Although highly motivated, hardworking, and extremely capable of adapting themselves in their new environment, they all must compete for a limited number of jobs in a highly competitive market. Housing also may be tight in the already overcrowded ghetto apartments of the cities or may be primitive in the poor shelters of the migrant worker camp.

As a result, ethnic peoples easily fall victim to hunger, housing, educational and health needs because of prejudice, discrimination, and social rejection. They are often educationally deprived and economically exploited. They need improved education, employment, and living conditions, as well as better treatment and greater acceptance.[4]

Once many immigrants begin to experience social mobility and a comfortable standard of living, however, the impact of American materialism undermines the traditional values of these otherwise happy and person-oriented ethnic people. The quest for material things leads to a breakdown in family life and to a susceptibility to all of America's social ills.[5]

It is in the midst of this instability and trauma that the church can minister effectively to the needs of the non-Christian ethnic immigrant. Food, clothing, and materials can be distributed by concerned Christians. Help can be given in locating affordable housing and in furnishing the new apartment. Conversational English and basic literacy classes can be sponsored by churches. The gospel will gain credibility as it is presented in the context of active, loving concern for the many peoples caught in the unfavorable social situations of this multicultural society.

SPIRITUAL CONDITION

Although most immigrants are religious, they have

great spiritual needs. Nevertheless, very few ethnics are having their spiritual condition addressed by the Anglo-American church, even though most are open to learning about Christianity and are highly responsive to the gospel message in their first year and a half after arriving in America.[6]

Many peoples in multi-ethnic America are nominally Roman Catholic. Statistically Hispanics and Haitians constitute twenty-five percent of the American Catholic Church, but most are not actively involved in church. Estimates indicate that more than eighty percent of Hispanics in the United States do not attend church and ever increasing numbers are flocking to other religious groups and cults.[7] The Anglo-American church needs to awaken to the fact that beneath the religious veneer of most ethnics of Roman Catholic background lie deep spiritual needs for the gospel which need to be met by an effective communication of God's message and love.

Numerous non-Christian religions, once thought to exist only in far off nations, are also embraced by many of America's ethnic peoples. These religions, complete with foreign-looking temples, idols, and rituals, are practiced by immigrants and are making converts of thousands of Americans.

Islam, followed by many Middle Easterner and some Asian peoples, has emerged in recent years as the fastest growing major religious tradition in the United States. Muslims constitute fourteen percent of the immigrants coming into America, and they now worship in more than six hundred Islamic centers across the country.[8] Muslims settle primarily in the larger cities but can be found in nearly every American town.

Christians have a unique opportunity to meet the spiritual need of Muslims who need to accept Jesus Christ as Lord and Savior by reaching out to the ethnics in their neighborhoods from Islamic countries.

Buddhists are other non-Christian religious practitioners who have immigrated to the United States in large numbers and blended into the multi-ethnic landscape of this nation. Southeast Asian, Japanese, and Chinese peoples adhere to the various sects of Buddhism. The meditation and mysticism of Buddhism has attracted many disenchanted Americans searching for a religious experience.

Hinduism is embraced by Asian Indian and Asian immigrants, and her adherents have erected several temples in the United States for the over one hundred thousand Hindus residing here. The Hare Krishna movement, Transcendental Meditation, and the New Age movement are visible influences of Hinduism on American society.[9]

The non-Christian religious traditions of many of America's ethnics pose a challenge to the church in America. Anglo churches need to recognize that some of the ethnics in their communities are from these religious backgrounds. Anglo-American Christians need to befriend these people, learn about their religions and cultures, attempt to understand them, and present the gospel to them in a way that is sensitive to their unique religious and cultural backgrounds.

These various geographic locations, social situations, and spiritual conditions of ethnic peoples comprise a part of the state of America's ethnic mosaic. Their needs, their difficulties, and their traumas present great opportunities to the Anglo-American church. Anglo-American Christians, who reach out with support, friendship, and a message of love to these millions that are adjusting to this new country, can favorably influence them with the gospel and can literally impact the world for Christ.

Endnotes

1. Parvin, *MissionsUSA*, p. 130.
2. Hadaway, "The People of a New Ethnic America," p. 46.
3. "Go West, Go East," *U.S. News and World Report*, 7 July 1986, pp. 30,31.
4. Etheredge, *Migrants*, p. 5
5. Montoya, *Hispanic Ministry in North America*, pp. 21-22.
6. Thomas and Arp, "How To Determine The Need For New Mission/Church Units," p. 7.
7. Parvin, *MissionsUSA*, p. 122.
8. Donald S. Tingle, "Islam Challenges The Church – What If The United States Became A Muslim Country?," 7 July 1986, Workshop, North American Christian Convention, Indianapolis, Indiana. (Printed.)
9. Parvin, *MissionsUSA*, pp. 171, 175, 176, 178.

PART TWO

WHAT KEEPS THE CHURCH FROM EVANGELIZING IN THE ETHNIC MOSAIC

NEGLECTING
THE BIBLICAL MANDATE

Jesus commanded His disciples to "go and make disciples of all nations" (Matt. 28:19 NIV). The Greek words from which "all nations" are translated have as their literal meaning "all ethnic groups." Because the Lord has commanded His followers to evangelize "all ethnic groups," those to be discipled, baptized, and taught to obey all the things that Jesus commanded His disciples will be a part of the mixture of ethnic groups in societies throughout the world.

Anglo-American Christians, therefore, cannot talk about evangelizing the United States without considering the non-Anglo populations in this multi-cultural nation. Today peoples with languages, cultural backgrounds, and religious traditions from around the world reside in this country. The Lord expects the church to be obedient enough to "go" to these multitudes within the borders of this multi-cultural nation and take advantage of this marvelous evangelistic opportunity in America's midst. The millions of ethnics in America are a mission field in this nation's backyard.

Nevertheless, too many Anglo-American Christians carelessly neglect the Biblical mandate. Many ethnic peoples move into their communities and come to be their neighbors, and yet they are indifferent to the way God sees others who are different from them, dismiss the Biblical example of reaching out to non-Anglos, and overlook their responsibility to share the gospel with other ethnics. These non-Anglo peoples may have heard something about Christ from a missionary in their home countries. However, in "Christian" America they no longer hear the message of God's reconciling love because Anglo-American Christians in the United States are not heeding Jesus' command to go and make disciples of them.

Too many churches in America have seen cross-cultural evangelism primarily in terms of geography, making the Anglo-American church blind to the unreached segments in this society which represent the unfinished evangelistic task in the United States. Anglo-American Christians have supported foreign missions in Mexico and Korea and yet have been unconcerned about the large Hispanic and Asian populations in their own communities.

A missionary dollar for cross-cultural evangelism does not become sacred when it crosses a geographic barrier. A distinction between cross-cultural missions in a foreign country and in the United States is not a Biblical concept. Moreover, appointing a missionary or a charitable organization to act as a proxy in cross-cultural outreach is insufficient for fulfilling the church's responsibility to Christ's commission. In this multi-cultural, multi-ethnic nation each Christian faces opportunities almost daily to relate cross-culturally in the name of Christ. Anglo-American Christians in America who are concerned about world evangelism cannot thoughtlessly ignore the Biblical directive to reach the transplanted foreign mission field which God has added to the ethnic make-up of this nation.

The Anglo-American church needs to realize that in the large pockets of unevangelized peoples in this nation God has placed at its doorstep one of the greatest opportunities for cross-cultural evangelism. Anglo Christians in the United States will be able to pay more careful attention to the winning of non-Anglos and will be able to keep from neglecting the mission directive to evangelize the multi-ethnic segments in American society by seeing ethnics in America the way God sees them, by remembering the Biblical example of evangelizing ethnics, and by carrying out their responsibility to those ethnics in this nation.

THE WAY GOD SEES ETHNICS

God created all peoples, each with their own peculiarities and differences. God sees each person in America's ethnic rainbow as a part of the world which He created and loves unconditionally (See John 3:16

and Deut. 10:18).

God's unconditional love for ethnic peoples is demonstrated by His provision for them in the Old Testament economy. Moses tells the Israelite community that "God loves the alien,[1] giving him food and clothing" (Deut. 10:18 NIV). The Psalmist recognizes God's provisional care for ethnics by stating that "the Lord watches over the alien" (Psalm 146:9 NIV). God's plan was to provide for the ethnic immigrant through the abundance of His blessings on the land and through the special tri-annual tithes (See Lev. 19:10 and Deut. 14:28,29).

In His justice, God also demonstrated His unconditional love for the ethnic immigrant by defending their cause in the face of ruthless oppressors. Through the prophet Malachi, the Lord promised to bring judgment against those who "deprive aliens of justice, but do not fear [Him]" (Mal. 3:15 NIV). Strong words of warning were used to impress the fact of God's protection for ethnics upon the minds of His people Israel, showing God's active concern for the welfare of peoples from other language or cultural groups.

The unconditional love of God for ethnic peoples, likewise, is demonstrated in the fact that He shows no favoritism to any one ethnic group. The Lord clearly told the Israelites that all people are equal in His eyes when He reminded them that "the Lord [their] God is God of gods and Lord of lords, the great God, mighty and awesome, who shows no partiality . . and loves the alien" (Deut. 10:17,18 NIV). After a miraculous vision showing that all people are to be recipients of the gospel, Peter learned that "God does not show favoritism but accepts men from every nation who fear him and do what is right" (Acts 10:34,35 NIV).

Because of His unconditional love for all ethnic peoples, God wants them to be drawn to Him through Jesus Christ and wants all barriers crossed to take the gospel to them. Orders given to Moses and the nation of Israel illustrate this reconciling love of God:

> Assemble the people – men, women, and children, and the aliens living in your towns – so they can listen and learn to fear the Lord your God and follow carefully all the words of this law. Their children, who do not know this law, must hear it and learn to fear the Lord your God as long as you live in the land you are crossing the Jordan to possess (Deut. 31:12,13 NIV).

The Lord's will to bring many peoples of all nations to Him also is aptly displayed in the Lord's commissioning words to His disciples in the Gospels and Acts (See Matt. 28:19,20, Mark 16:15, Luke 24:46-48, John 20:21, and Acts 1:8).

Anglo-American Christians will remain careless in the evangelization of America and will neglect the Lord's charge to reach out with the gospel to all segments of this multi-cultural nation if they fail to view the ethnic immigrants in America's midst the way God does. God loves ethnic peoples by providing for them, by defending their interests, by showing no partiality, and by seeking to reconcile Himself to them through the gospel of Christ. If the Anglo-American church in the United States recognizes God's unconditional love for ethnic peoples in this nation, it will actively participate in the evangelization of this country's ethnic mosaic.

BIBLICAL EXAMPLE OF EVANGELIZING ETHNICS

The Bible consistently records God's love and concern for all the nations of the world and God's desire for His people to be instruments by which the message of God's love would be proclaimed to all nations. In His promise to Abraham God said: "All peoples on earth will be blessed through you" (Gen. 12:3 NIV). Isaiah noted that the nation of Israel was to bring the message of the living God and the hope of the Messiah to the world: "I will keep you and will make you to be a covenant for the people and a light for the Gentiles" (Isa. 42:6 NIV).

Jesus reaffirmed this evangelistic directive before His ascension, stating that the scope of this task of bearing witness was to be "in Jerusalem and in all Judea and Samaria and to the end of the earth" (Acts 1:8 NIV). From the very day that the church was born on Pentecost, the disciples of Jesus were faced with the challenge of evangelizing in cities flooded with ethnic peoples of different languages, cultures, and religious traditions (Acts 2:5 NIV). The early church confronted missionary opportunities of world- wide scope from the first day of its existence and proclaimed the gospel to these diverse peoples.

Of course, that global perspective on evangelism did not come easily for those early disciples. The gospel first took root only among the Jews and Jewish converts from the nations of the world since many Christians spoke only to Jews (Acts 11:19 NIV). Early church history in the book of Acts recounts the great difficulty the church had in breaking through the cultural barriers to the Samaritans and finally to the Gentiles. Luke, however, closes his account in Acts with the gospel of Christ being available to all peoples.

The Biblical pattern of crossing cultural barriers to evangelize peoples from every ethnic group is also God's pattern for His church today. Nevertheless, Anglo-American Christians at the end of the Twentieth Century easily find excuses to dismiss the Biblical example of evangelizing all ethnic groups and tend to turn inward to their own kind of people. The cultural barriers which must be crossed to the ethnics from the nations of the world still present the greatest difficulty to churches in America.

Anglo-American churches will leave undone the Lord's command to reach non-Anglos in the United States with the gospel if they fail to remember the Biblical example to evangelize all peoples. Hundreds of ethnic groups which have not heard the message of Christ reside in this nation. Churches in this country will actively participate in the evangelization of the ethnic mosaic if American Christians follow the Biblical example of cross-cultural communications of the gospel to ethnic peoples and recapture the commitment of the New Testament church to carry the good news of God to all the world.

ANGLO-AMERICAN CHRISTIANS' RESPONSIBILITY TO ETHNICS

Anglo-American churches in the United States often fail to reach out to the diverse peoples of this multi-cultural nation because Anglo Christians unthinkingly

RED & YELLOW, BLACK & WHITE...

neglect the Lord's charge to His people to proclaim the gospel to all ethnic groups. Although they recognize their responsibility to reach the lost in this society with Jesus' love, Anglo-American Christians find it easier to turn inward, to seek their own kind, and thus to become exclusive in their sharing of the gospel.

In their exclusiveness, Anglo-American Christians feel uncomfortable with other types of people and avoid friendships or association with those from different cultures. In the midst of the varied cultures in America, many of them are isolated. They are threatened by people who are not like themselves and, thus, relate only to people like themselves. As individuals or as churches, Anglo Christians build a wall, finding it easier to write off the different people in their communities and to excuse themselves from visiting non-Anglos and inviting them to follow Jesus. Anglo-American Christians or churches which limit their witness for Christ and become exclusive for any reason are neglecting the Lord's command to proclaim the gospel to all ethnic groups and are declaring an unwillingness to accept their Biblical responsibility to reach out to the vast assortment of ethnic groups in this country.

Instead of an exclusiveness, Anglo-American congregations need to maintain a commitment to include all segments of their communities in the proclamation of the gospel. As neighborhoods change, churches need to choose to have a vision of reaching everyone in that community and of remaining with a testimony of the gospel to the residents of their neighborhoods no matter who they happen to be.

The Apostle Paul saw his responsibility to witness to

everyone he met, regardless of who they were. He expressed his inclusive intent in this way:

> Though I am free and belong to no man, I make myself a slave to everyone, to win as many as possible. To the Jews I became like a Jew, to win the Jews. To those under the law I became like one under the law (though I myself am not under the law), so as to win those under the law. To those not having the law I became like one not having the law (though I am not free from God's law but am under Christ's law), so as to win those not having the law. To the weak I became weak, to win he weak. I have become all things to all men so that by all possible means I might save some (I Cor. 9:19-22 NIV).

Christians are meant to be inclusive in their proclamation of the gospel. The Christian faith is not limited to one language or culture and needs to be shared in as many cultures and languages as exist in a church's neighborhood and as are found in America. Any exclusiveness, intentional or by default, neglects the Biblical responsibility to reach out to whomever the Lord brings into this country and its communities.

In addition to the responsibility for Anglo-American Christians to have an inclusive intent in outreach to the ethnics in their neighborhoods, Christians in this nation have a Biblical responsibility to love ethnics. Moses' words to the nation of Israel serve as a Scriptural cornerstone for Christians in the United States today:

> When an alien lives with you in your land, do not mistreat him. The alien living with you must be treated as one of your native-born. Love him as yourself, . . . (Lev. 19:33,34 NIV).

God's clear intention for His people is that they love the ethnic peoples who live in their midst. Anglo-American Christians need to recognize the personal worth of all ethnic peoples in God's sight and to accept their Biblical responsibility to love them.

People of ethnic groups, cultures, and languages should be the objects of the Anglo-American church's tender compassion and love. God has given Anglo Christians the responsibility to love a non-Anglo person as one born among them and as themselves. The Anglo-American church is to love them and become involved in their world because they are ones for whom Jesus died. An outreach ministry into the multi-cultural fabric of this nation is a living expression of that active love.

Besides responsibly exhibiting an inclusive intent and an active love, Anglo-American Christians should open their homes to those from non-Anglo backgrounds. A Biblical exhortation on the church's attitude to ethnics in its midst states, "Do not forget to entertain strangers, for by so doing some people have entertained angels without knowing it" (Heb. 13:2 NIV). Perhaps non-Christian neighbors do not care for the non-Anglos in America's communities, but a Christian's responsibility is clear. He or she must practice hospitality.

Lamentably, peoples in the United States from non-Anglo-Saxon and non-Protestant cultural, language, and religious backgrounds have not always experienced Christian hospitality and genuine Christian love and have returned to their homelands soured to Christianity and the gospel. On the other hand, however, kind treatment and warm hospitality toward ethnics has potential for incalculable benefits for the name of the

Lord and His Kingdom around the world. Anglo-American Christians need to remember their responsibility to show hospitality to all peoples who live in this nation.

Another important responsibility to America's ethnic peoples is a commitment to vigorous outreach, not simply a sympathetic tolerance of ethnic participation in Anglo-American churches. Some Anglo congregations point with some pride to the fact that they "allow" ethnics to worship with them or that they have a genuine desire to have or support a multi-ethnic congregation.

Nevertheless, more than a passive tolerance of an ethnic presence is required. An active attempt to establish relationships with their ethnic neighbors and reach them with the gospel needs to be made by Anglo-American churches. The Biblical responsibility is clear when Paul states:

> How, then, can they call on the one they have not believed in? And how can they believe in the one of whom they have not heard? And how can they hear without someone preaching to them? And how can they preach unless they are sent? As it is written, "How beautiful are the feet of those who bring good news" (Rom. 10:14,15 NIV)!

Anglo-American Christians must pledge more vigorous support to ethnic evangelism if everyone in this nation is to hear the message of God's reconciling love and if the church in America is to remain true to Jesus' command to share the gospel with all peoples. The Anglo church can no longer feel fulfilled in paying for mission work to be done by others or in supporting evangelistic efforts that bypass those in the numerous ethnic groups of America. Instead, the Anglo church must develop a larger vision of its responsibility to energetically reach out in the area of ethnic evangelism.

Anglo-American churches will fail to carry out the Biblical directive to reach ethnics in the United States if they overlook the Biblical responsibility toward the ethnics who are among them. The responsibility of the Anglo Church is to inclusively take the gospel message to whomever the Lord brings into its neighborhood. The responsibility of the Anglo church is to love non-Anglos and show them hospitality. The responsibility of the Anglo is to vigorously proclaim to them the gospel message. The church's Biblical responsibility compels it to love America's ethnic peoples and to faithfully bring the gospel to all ethnic groups in this nation.

The Anglo-American church is often kept from evangelizing millions of this nation's people because it unthinkingly neglects the Biblical mandate to bring the gospel to all ethnic groups. The unreached in multi-cultural America often live side-by-side with Anglo-American Christians. Believers in this country need to awaken to the desperate need to obey God's command to His church to preach the gospel to "all" peoples.

Anglo-American Christians need to view non-Anglos in the United States the way God does – with unconditional love. Anglo-American Christians in the United States need to follow the Biblical example of taking the gospel cross-culturally to ethnic units in this society and need to recapture the commitment of taking the gospel to all peoples both here and abroad. Anglo-American Christians need to recognize their responsibility to live out God's love and to actively reach out evangelistically among the potpourri of ethnic peoples in this nation. Obedience to the Lord's command in each of these areas will enable the American church to begin to effectively make disciples of all ethnic groups within this nation's ethnic mosaic.

Endnotes

1. The ethnic immigrants in the Old Testament who lived among the Israelites were referred to as "aliens," "strangers," and "sojourners."

GIVING WAY TO FEAR

The diversity of languages and cultures has been created by God, and these differences of people make the communities in the United States and the societies around the world more interesting and exciting places to live. Anglo-American Christians travel across this great land and to other countries of the world to discover the lifestyles of various people, to examine their thinking, to experiment with their culinary delights, and to see their native dress.

In the midst of these varied cultures in the communities of America, however, many Anglo-American Christians turn inward and seek their own kind, remaining isolated from a world that the church has been commanded to penetrate. In distant lands these ethnic peoples receive their missionary efforts and concern. But in America's neighborhoods diverse ethnic groups threaten Anglo-American Christians, and these Christians give way to fear.

This fear causes Anglo-American Christians to build a wall between them and their diverse ethnic neighbors, and they find it easier to write off the others in their communities who are different than they are. Because they are afraid, Anglo-American Christians relate only to people like themselves and, thus severely limit their witness in the ethnic mosaic. Fear keeps them from evangelizing this multi-cultural nation.

Every community in the United States is experiencing the changes which the ever-growing potpourri of ethnic peoples is bringing to this country. Every church is faced with the challenge of surrendering to nervous bias concerning America's ethnic presence and of succumbing to the negative attitudes which accompany those phobias. Nevertheless, Anglo-American Christians need to overcome these fears and reach out to whomever the Lord brings into their neighborhoods. This can be done by examining their hearts for fears and prejudice, by facing any phobias and prejudice and asking God to remove them from their lives, and by recognizing the positive attitudes which are essential for accepting the challenge of winning their various ethnic neighbors to Christ.

FEARS WHICH HINDER EVANGELISM

This world is very conscious of the difference in

people, and individuals have a strong natural tendency
to seek the security of their own kind of people. Deep
down inside, all people are afraid of that which is different. The fear of diversity often causes Anglo-American
Christians to avoid friendships with non-Anglos who
are different and to rationalize comfortable relationships with one's own kind. Most people are comfortable
around those individuals who have largely the same
behavior and values, but they are ill at ease with people
from diverse backgrounds and cultures which differ in
many ways.[1]

This apprehension about diversity has caused much
harm to the outreach ministry of the Anglo-American
church to non-Anglos. Some Anglo churches have taken
pride in their Anglo heritage, insisting that the ethnic
peoples outside Anglo culture "become like them" by
learning English and adopting Anglo ways in order to
hear the gospel. Other congregations have opened their
doors to the various peoples in their neighborhoods,
allowing them to attend but not actively going after
them. Still additional churches have embarked upon
sincere efforts to integrate cultures into a multi-ethnic
worshiping congregation, failing to realize the powerful
influence of culture and language upon an ethnic person's individual and group behavior.

Diversity is ordained by God and brings beauty to the
society in which one lives. Nevertheless, the fear of
diversity hinders the Anglo-American church's attempt
to evangelize this multi-cultural society.

The fear of the unfamiliar also hinders the evangelization of America's non-Anglo population. Languages
and cultures that are unfamiliar often trigger irrita-

tions and misunderstandings by Anglo-American Christians toward their non-Anglo neighbors because these uncertainties require adjustments in the way Anglo-Americans are used to behaving and responding.

An Anglo-American Christian's attitude toward the unfamiliar has traditionally been to insist that other ethnic peoples learn English and adapt to the Anglo-American way of doing things. With the salvation of millions of souls at stake, however, this thinking that non-Anglos need to give up their ethnic distinctiveness and conform to Anglo-American norms in order to become Christians severely limits the possibility of many ethnics being able to hear and appropriate the gospel in a language and culture with which they are most familiar and comfortable.

Many Anglo-American Christians, likewise, allow the fear of change to hinder the witness among the mixture of ethnic groups in America. When ethnic peoples begin to move into the Anglo-American community, members of the church are afraid of what will happen to their neighborhood and church. These changes in the ethnic composition of the community come to be viewed as something to resist, and the dread of losing the neighborhood's identity creates pressure to oppose the new residents or to flee the instability which the changes bring. [2]

The white fright brought on by these changing ethnic patterns often leads to a white flight from the community or to a retreat into a ministry which has no vision for reaching the lost among the church's ethnic neighbors. This phobia concerning change keeps many Anglo-American Christians from making provisions for the evangelization of all those whom God brings into this country and its communities.

The fear of diversity, the fear of the unfamiliar, and the fear of change all become hindrances to communicating the love of Jesus to all peoples. If left unchecked, these fears can give rise to negative attitudes which lead to prejudice.

PREJUDICE

Exclusiveness is one negative attitude which accompanies fear and contributes to prejudice. Some Anglo-American Christians are quick to vocalize their openness to all groups and individuals yet are slow to actively reach out to all people in demonstrable ways. Although many churches never officially exclude anyone, they never vigorously include everyone. The "whiteness" of many churches reveals the years of inactivity in the area of ethnic evangelism.[3]

If Anglo-American Christians do nothing to reach out to non-Anglos, it displays prejudice just as boldly as publicly making ethnic slurs in church meetings would. A passive exclusiveness fails to demonstrate the love of Christ to other ethnic neighbors and reinforces the barriers of prejudice which exist in many American communities.

An exclusiveness in the form of segregation is found in some churches, and this form of prejudice has been tolerated too long in the church. Some Anglo-American Christians believe that people of different cultures and races should be kept separated, and fellowship between the various groups is strongly discouraged.[4] This segregation maligns God's name and church. Such exclusiveness damages relationships with ethnic neighbors and destroys bridges for the gospel into ethnic communities.

White flight is an exclusiveness which is alive and well in some Anglo-American churches. Some Christians across America are living in neighborhoods which are experiencing an influx of various ethnic groups and are neglecting to reach out to these newcomers. Homes and church buildings are being sold by Christians when the community begins to change ethnically, and these Christians are moving to the suburbs with no provision for an evangelistic witness in the vacated community. This retreat is a form of prejudice because it indicates no long-term commitment nor vision for sharing the gospel to the residents of a neighborhood regardless of their ethnic, linguistic, or racial heritage.

Exclusiveness is an unbiblical response to the ethnic presence in a community. Many Anglo-American Christians and churches need to face up to this prejudice and to deal with their passive exclusiveness, their segregation, and their white flight. Any exclusiveness and prejudice will keep the Anglo-American church from openly proclaiming the gospel to all peoples in this multi-cultural nation.

Cultural pride is also a negative attitude which accompanies fear and contributes to prejudice. This prideful way of thinking causes Anglo-American Christians to speak of non-Anglos as "them" and all Anglos as "us," ignoring the fact that white, Anglo-Saxon Americans are an ethnic grouping which is a minority in the world. This ethnocentric view says, "My way is the right way or the only way," or "You are different (which means 'you are wrong')." Such cultural elitism is prejudice because it demands conformity of any newcomers, expresses itself in paternalistic ways, and tends to think that no other ethnic people is as good as one's own group.[5]

This culture-centeredness becomes a barrier to communicating the gospel of Christ to multi-cultural America. From God's perspective, no ideal culture exists. People are not inferior because they are different from Anglo-Americans. Anglo-American Christians in the United States need to get rid of any cultural pride and eliminate any part of Anglo-American culture that keeps the church from accepting all cultural and ethnic groups and reaching out to them with the love of Christ.

Stereotyping, likewise, is a negative attitude which accompanies fear and contributes to prejudice. In stereotyping, members of a group have preconceived attitudes, opinions, and beliefs about members of another nation or ethnic group and insist on these standardized generalities and preconceptions of people in a particular group. This tendency to think in national or ethnic stereotypes is not limited to any one nation or ethnic group, and Anglo-American Christians are just as inclined as any ethnic group to apply stereotypes or labels.[6]

Although an ethnic group's traits are often too complex to reduce to one homogeneous list of characteristics, Anglo-American Christians frequently write off different peoples in this multi-cultural society with stereotyped generalizations. The Anglo-American church often expresses that non-Anglos are not responsible people, do not want to associate with Anglos, are not interested in Christianity, or will not let the church help them. This stereotyping passes judgment on another ethnic group in order to justify keeping separated from these people who are different, and it leads to a judgmental attitude.

Communication of the gospel is hindered by stereotyping because it reinforces pride and prejudice, clings to preconceived labels, and supports a negligent posture toward an evangelization of non-Anglos in America. Anglo-American Christians need to recognize that they are frequently in bondage to stereotypes. They need to put an end to passing judgment on an entire ethnic group because of preconceived opinions or values. Relating to people from different nations and cultures on an individual basis will help eliminate the prejudice from stereotyping and will serve to facilitate any active proclamation of the gospel among America's distinctive ethnic groups.

Exclusiveness, cultural pride, and stereotyping are negative attitudes which accompany fear and contribute to prejudice. Anglo-American Christians need to realize any hidden fears and hostile feelings which they embrace and which are often theologically justified in their churches. Then, they can attempt to eliminate any negative attitudes and can begin to concentrate on developing the positive attitudes which are needed to overcome fear and prejudice.

OVERCOMING FEAR AND PREJUDICE

If fears are faced openly and prejudice is dealt with

honestly, Anglo-American Christians will recognize that they naturally prefer their own culture and are threatened by too much change. They will realize their need to deliberately and purposefully break out of their culture to reach the ethnic communities around them with the gospel.

Although the group identity and preference which Anglo-American Christians and all ethnic peoples have is a positive aspect of human life, Anglo-American Christians need to be willing to risk losing the comfort of their own kind to take the gospel to non-Anglos in this multi-cultural nation. Plans, therefore, should be made to deliberately and energetically put Christians in contact with individuals from cultures and languages that are different. Recognizing they prefer their own kind and breaking out of their comfortable situations will contribute to Anglo-American Christians' ability to overcome fear and prejudice.

Along with realizing their preference for people like themselves and their need to interact with other cultures, Anglo-American Christians need to acknowledge the worth of all people before God and to share the message of Christ in multi-cultural America, if fear and prejudice are to be overcome. Although the church is frequently quick to vocalize a respect for the contribution of every culture, in practice Anglo-American Christians are slow to demonstrate an active and realistic outreach to peoples who are from different languages and cultural backgrounds.

Anglo-American Christians need to determine what can be realistically done to reach the total community and to proclaim about salvation in Jesus Christ to all the ethnic peoples in America's neighborhoods. This will halt any hindrance which fear and prejudice can bring to the spread of the gospel among all peoples in America and will facilitate cross-cultural outreach to their ethnic neighbors (See I Cor. 9:19-22).

Of course, any active outreach of this nature will need to be done in a spirit of humility. Christian witness has often been a form of Christian imperialism where pride and insensitivity have hindered the church's testimony, have placed a barrier in the way of people responding to the gospel, and have contributed to the resistance of many peoples to the message which is proclaimed.

Cross-cultural evangelism necessitates humility. The customs, culture, and language of ethnic people should be accepted as being perfectly legitimate. Anglo-American Christians need to be willing to be taught by people of different cultures, listening sensitively to them and learning humbly from them. As Anglo-American Christians unpretentiously communicate concern and acceptance, fear and prejudice will be overcome, and the message of the gospel will more likely be heard by peoples from languages, cultural backgrounds, and religious heritages which are different from the dominant Anglo-American culture.

The key attitude which will make it possible for the Anglo-American church to risk the comfortable, to recognize the value of everyone, and to relate unassumingly is love. Christians who love only those who are like them fall short of God's ideal love and compassion for all men. The church must resolve to love everyone as God loves (See John 15:13 and I John 3:16). God's love needs to motivate and dominate the witness of Anglo-

American Christians to the non-Anglos in this nation.

Christian men and women need to walk among their ethnic neighbors as those who live God's reconciling love. They do this by serving the needs of those of different cultural groups, by setting aside the time for meaningful personal contact with their ethnic neighbors, and by sharing their lives in interdependence with the ethnic community. God's love is still the most effective way to overcome fear and prejudice and to share the gospel in this multi-cultural nation.

Instead of giving way to fear, Anglo-American Christians need to deliberately and vigorously reach out to ethnic America with the gospel. Even though examples of the Anglo-American church's negligence in reaching all peoples abound, a change to positive attitudes among Christians toward peoples of different cultures and languages is beginning to come slowly. If breaking out of the comfortable succeeds, if valuing all cultures prevails, if humbly interacting with ethnics exists, and if loving others motivates and dominates, then Anglo-American Christians will no longer yield to negative attitudes and be overcome by prejudice, and Anglo-American churches will succeed in the evangelization of the ethnic mosaic.

Endnotes

1. James Duren and Rod Wilson, *The Stranger Who Is Among You* (Pasadena, CA: William Carey Library, 1983), pp. 8-12.

2. Belew, "Introduction," p. 6.

3. James Westgate, "When the World Arrives on Your Doorstep," in *Heirs of the Same Promise*, ed. Wesley D. Balda (Ar-

cadia, CA: National Convocation on Evangelizing Ethnic America, 1984), pp. 76-77.

4. Montoya, *Hispanic Ministry in North America*, p. 78.

5. Duren and Wilson, *The Stranger Who Is Among You*, pp. 8-10.

6. Lau, *The World At Your Doorstep*, pp. 52-54.

LINGERING IN PROVINCIALISM

Thousands of Anglo-American churches in the United States today support an army of missionaries and a host of mission and benevolent organizations overseas. However, in spite of various endeavors in world missions, many of these churches tend to be rather provincial in their thinking about the evangelization of America and, thus, fail to penetrate the unreached segments of this nation's multi-cultural urban centers. Because most Anglo-American churches are located in agrarian or suburban communities and maintain a small town approach to their ministry styles, they are unsuccessful at breaking out of a mono-cultural-centeredness and a rural bias and at reaching and evangelizing the ethnic mosaic that is found in

111

America's cities.

Urban ethnic ministry is one of the greatest challenges of world missions today and yet one of the greatest failures. The rural nature of the Anglo-American church not only blinds Anglo Christians to the fact that the multi-cultural fabric of American society demands crossing cultural barriers to reach a multitude of ethnic groups with the gospel, but it also causes them to overlook the urban centers of the nation which are home to the majority of America's population, including ethnics.

Although the rate of urbanization has slowed in the past few years, over three quarters of all Americans live in metropolitan areas,[1] with over ninety percent of non-Anglo peoples dwelling in cities.[2] In the cities, unchurched urbanites are pressed together in an environment where they are nearly as isolated from the preaching of the gospel as peoples in many countries of the world. Actually, the number of people in the urban areas of the United States who are lost and in need of evangelization is exceeded only by the population of China, India, the Soviet Union, and Indonesia.[3]

Too often Anglo-American churches neglect the need for cross-cultural mission outreach among the various ethnic groups that dwell in the modern, socially complex centers of this nation because Christians are largely rural in their orientation and are inattentive to the microcosm of the world in America's cities. A rainbow of languages, colors, and cultural traditions are found in urban America, which means that the mission outreach of the church in America must include the cities if lost ethnic peoples are going to be won to the

Lord Jesus Christ. If the Anglo-American church is to emerge from its lingering provincialism and to penetrate the multi-cultural world of this nation's urban centers, Christians need to recognize the ethnic presence in the cities, to acknowledge the church's past ineffectiveness in evangelizing non-Anglos in urban centers, and to capture a vision for urban America so that all peoples in America have an opportunity to respond to the gospel.

THE ETHNIC PRESENCE IN CITIES

Anglo-American Christians need to recognize that the church should not guard its rural heritage at the expense of urban evangelism because the ethnic presence in the urban centers of the United States is undeniable. Newly arriving ethnics from around the world are settling in the cities, and old urban neighborhoods are retaining cultures that are unique to their homelands. Moving in with them are Native Americans who can no longer find employment in rural America and who are now more numerous in urban areas than on reservations.[4] America's cities are clusters of hundreds of different ethnic groups that are separated from each other by invisible barriers of language, culture, and economics.

In less than ten years, more than fifty major American cities will be predominantly ethnic, and numerous metropolitan areas will be some of the largest non-Anglo centers in the world. Already New York City has more Puerto Ricans than anywhere but San Juan,

Miami more Cubans than anywhere but Havana, Chicago more Poles than anywhere but Warsaw, Los Angeles more Hispanics than anywhere in the Western Hemisphere but Mexico City, and Brooklyn more Haitians than anywhere but Port-au-Prince.[5] And while the central cities are growing in their ethnic populations, the suburban fringes are also quietly and steadily becoming more culturally diverse.

Historically, the majority of non-Anglos have been drawn to the cities. The immigrants of the late Nineteenth and early Twentieth Centuries were largely Europeans who found jobs in America's growing cities. Most of today's immigrants come from Asia and Latin America out of political or economic necessity and are taking over the middle class neighborhoods of the city which are being vacated by the Anglo population.[6] Like a magnet, the American city is attracting ethnic peoples from across the globe.

Over the decades most of these immigrants have settled in this nation's cities because the urban ethnic community offered them groups of people with whom they could identify, markets where ethnic foods could be purchased, neighbors who spoke their languages, friends who maintained their distinct cultural patterns, and social structures which met religious, emotional, and personal needs. This tendency to urbanize changed the nation's cities in dramatic and unexpected ways and created populations that are culturally mixed and ethnically diverse.[7]

Although this shift to an urban and ethnic population challenges the church to break out of its rural orientation and to take the gospel of Christ to the city,

Anglo-American Christians still have little or no out-reach among these teeming millions and largely continue to be ineffective in reaching America's multi-ethnic urban centers. Several reasons exist for the tenacity of ruralism in the Anglo-American church and for its unsuccessful attempts at reaching the urban ethnic community.

THE LACK OF SUCCESS IN
REACHING ETHNICS IN THE CITY

Anglo-American Christians have been ineffective in reaching ethnics in this nation's cities because many Anglo-American churches are rural in location and mind-set. Traditionally agrarian, middle class, and Anglo, most churches in America have been strong in the smaller communities in the heartland of the nation and have reached only suburbanites like themselves.[8] Breaking out beyond the traditional rural and suburban strength into the new frontier of urban evangelism will require that numerous Anglo churches in America go to great lengths to include all ethnic groups, to remain in ethnically-changing neighborhoods, and to reach out energetically with the gospel to America's diverse ethnic peoples.

The largely unsuccessful efforts at reaching the urban ethnic community have also been exacerbated by the insistence that English be the standard language for the American church. This stipulation, prompted by the Anglo-American church's rural experience, has resulted in urban congregations where the praying, preaching, and singing are all done in English and where many people struggle in a language which they imperfectly understand. In cities which are made up of many peoples and many languages, preaching of the gospel is bound to be misunderstood and church planting frustrated if English language is a condition for proclaiming or hearing the message of Christ.[9]

Learning other languages will be required for effective proclamation of the gospel in America's multi-cultural cities. Successful outreach to the ethnic communities in the metropolitan centers will necessitate urban ministries in as many languages as are spoken in America.

Likewise, the Anglo-American church has been ineffective in reaching the non-Anglos in cities because of an attitude of neglect on the part of Christians. Most Anglo-American Christians know that other ethnic peoples should be loved by them, but they are more comfortable doing so from a distance, ministering only to their own kind of people.[10] A heart burden for the individuals without Christ among the diverse ethnic groups in America's cities can move Anglo-American Christians out of this complacency and into action. An active concern for the lost in the numerous ethnic enclaves of the city can help them recapture a vision for urban America.

The negative image of the city has also contributed to faltering efforts by Anglo-American Christians to reach urban ethnics. Churches in the city have been known for poor growth and for limited moral and religious impact on the unchurched urbanites. Since many churches have been unable to make much lasting impression on

American cities, Anglo-American Christians have retreated from the great urban centers, convinced that urban ethnic ministry is too difficult and barren.[11]

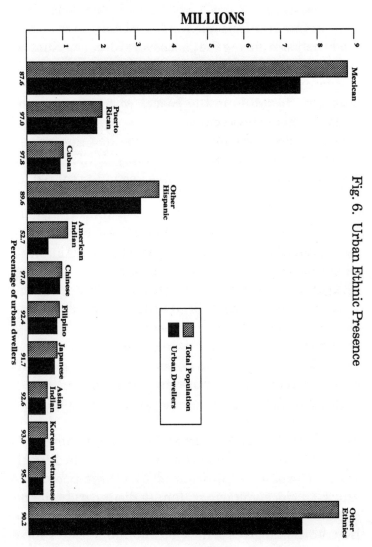

Fig. 6. Urban Ethnic Presence

Changing the view of Anglo-American Christians toward urban ministry and improving the Anglo-American church's urban endeavors will require that the church assume responsibility for its lack of success at assimilating ethnic peoples and remaining in changing neighborhoods during the past several decades. Success in sharing the gospel with non-Anglos will necessitate that rural and suburban Anglo-American churches determine to proclaim the gospel with power on the streets of this nation's cities.

The Anglo-American church also has not accomplished the evangelization of the many ethnic groups in this nation's cities because it has been ill-prepared for and incapable of dealing effectively with constantly changing ethnic communities.[12] Anglo-American Christians have lacked an urban strategy which can adequately reach the multitude of cultures in America's urban centers and, as a result, have fostered weak and struggling ministries among urban ethnics. If the Anglo-American church is to grow beyond rural and suburban America and reach non-Anglos, it needs to identify and study the thousands of ethnically diverse groups in the cities and to devise urban strategies that will effectively lead to their evangelization.[13]

The church's ineffectiveness among urban ethnics, likewise, has resulted from a lack of preparation for the problems in the city. Non-urban Christians in America's Anglo churches often have not understood the difficulties and problems confronted by ethnic peoples.[14] Drugs, suicides, muggings, family disintegration, and loneliness – all part of city life – have been destructive to the traditional lives which ethnic immigrants have known.[15] An urban secularism and a callousness toward sin have created a moral and spiritual climate not easily addressed by a traditionally rural church.[16] A penetration of the gospel into metropolitan areas will be possible when the church develops a viable and relevant Biblical response to the moral and social questions which face ethnics in the city.

The rural background of Anglo-American churches also has contributed to an abandonment of the city because of an inability or unwillingness to adapt to the changing urban neighborhoods. In fleeing to the suburbs during the past decades, most churches left no provision for a witness to the different ethnic groups which remained behind.[17] As a result of white flight, suburban Anglo-American churches found themselves ill-equipped and at a disadvantage for sharing the gospel with the various ethnic groups left in the cities. Resisting the temptation to sell or dissolve urban churches, developing a vision for reaching the ethnic groups in changing urban communities, and establishing credible evangelistic urban ministries outside suburbia and small towns will be necessary for effectively evangelizing the non-Anglos in America's cities.

An unwillingness to pay the price for ethnic evangelism in urban centers also has caused Anglo-American Christians to be ineffective in reaching America's multiethnic cities. Anglo-Americans shun failure and prize success. Ethnic evangelism in the city is laden with hardships. Fruitful ministry is not easily measured by budgets, buildings, and attendance figures.[18] As a result, gifted workers have often been drawn away to the challenges of higher salaries and bigger churches, leaving the ethnic church in the city without adequate workers, money, or expertise. A failure to sacrifice for the evangelization of the non-Anglo peoples in urban America will only be overcome by a redefinition of success in the Kingdom and by a commitment to the challenge of ethnic urban ministry.

A small-town mentality has persisted among Anglo-American Christians. Ethnic ministry in America's cities has remained ineffective because of a rural mind set, an English language standard, an attitude of neglect toward the evangelization of non-Anglos, a negative image of the city, an absence of an urban strategy, a lack of planning for urban problems, an abandonment of the city, and an unwillingness to pay the price of urban ministry. Anglo-American Christians can leave their ruralism behind and overcome these barriers to the evangelization of all peoples if the church focuses on the needs of urban ethnics and the opportunities for reaching them with the gospel.

CAPTURING A VISION FOR URBAN AMERICA

In order to capture a vision for the evangelization of urban America, Anglo-American Christians need to recognize that urban ethnics represent the most approachable, needy, and often most receptive group of unreached people at this time.[19] Uprooted and transplanted ethnic peoples, getting a new start in life and needing friendship and a sense of belonging, have moved into this nation's cities. These newly arriving immigrants frequently are separated from the close control of family and social structures and have left behind their intimate tie to religious beliefs and practices. Consequently, they can be reached and are very open to the gospel.[20]

Realizing the potential and receptivity of the ethnic peoples in the cities, the Anglo church in America needs to develop a goal for advancing the Kingdom to the urban communities through the starting of Bible studies and planting of ethnic churches in other languages. New church evangelism can work as well in reaching particular ethnic groups in the city as in evangelizing high growth suburban areas.[21]

Anglo-American Christians, therefore, need to launch out with the gospel in each and every ethnic group in the city, helping them to be like Christ in their own language and cultural form. The life, vitality, and excitement of a multitude of newly planted ethnic churches in the city will hasten the gospel to this multicultural nation and will do much to revive the mono-cultural Anglo-American church.

Capturing a vision for urban America can lead to the worldwide proclamation of the gospel and to the global expansion of the church to the relatives of ethnic Americans in distant nations. Obviously, an evangelistic ministry which reaches the mixture of ethnic groups in America cities can develop and train national workers who will require little adjustment to carry that gospel message back to the lost in their homeland countries.[22] Indeed, thriving ethnic churches in urban America can provide bridges to the evangelization of the world.

The spiritual needs of non-Anglos in urban America face the Anglo church in the United States as urgently as the multitudes on the foreign mission fields of the world. Millions of unreached ethnic people in the towering apartments, the neighborhood slums, and the crowded communities of American cities wait for the message and hope of the gospel of Christ.

Reaching ethnics in America for Christ means sharing the gospel in the urban centers of this nation. The time has come for Anglo-American Christians in this country to acknowledge the ethnic presence in their cities, to recognize the lack of evangelistic success among urban ethnics in the past, and to capture a vision for the sharing the gospel in urban America. Certainly, nothing less than the winning of America is at stake in taking the gospel to urban ethnics.

Each generation of Christians is faced with new evangelistic responsibilities, opportunities, and challenges. Truly, the greatest challenge for Christians in the 1990's is to emerge from its lingering provincialism and to learn to relate the gospel effectively across cultural differences and in urban settings to the ethnic mosaic in America.

Endnotes

1. Parvin, *MissionsUSA*, p. 248.
2. "The Newest Markets for New Churches," *Visionary*, June 1989, p. 3.
3. Parvin, *MissionsUSA*, p. 268.
4. Home Mission Board, *Language Mission Facts*, p. 8.
5. Roger S. Greenway and Timothy M. Monsma, *Cities: Mission's New Frontier* (Grand Rapids, MI: Baker Book House, 1989), pp. 62,63.
6. Roger S. Greenway, "The Shift to Ethnic Mission," *The Mandate*, March 1985, p. 1.

7. Greenway and Monsma, *Cities*, p. 63.

8. "Who Will Win America?" *MissionsUSA,* March/April 1987, p. 9.

9. Donald McGavran, *Understanding Church Growth* (Grand Rapids, MI: William B. Eerdmans Publishing Company, 1970), pp. 289,290.

10. Greenway and Monsma, *Cities*, p. 73.

11. Ibid., pp. 73,74.

12. Parvin, *MissionsUSA*, p. 44.

13. Roger S. Greenway, "Reaching the Unreached in the Cities," *The Mandate,* October 1985, p. 14.

14. Duren and Wilson, *The Stranger Who Is Among You,* p. 20.

15. Nelson L. Deuitch, "Toronto – The Meeting Place," *Christian Standard,* 28 January 1990, p. 12.

16. Greenway and Monsma, *Cities*, p. 75.

17. Parvin, *MissionsUSA*, pp. 275,276.

18. Jim Spicer, "What I Have Learned From Thirteen Years Of Working in an Integrated Church and Neighborhood," workshop given at the North American Christian Convention, Indianapolis, IN, 8 July 1986. (Photocopied.)

19. Greenway, "Reaching the Unreached in the Cities," p. 14.

20. McGavran, *Understanding Church Growth*, p. 282.

21. Roger Boatman, "The Mission Field Has Come Home," *The Lookout,* 23 March 1980, p. 7.

22. Greenway and Monsma, *Cities,* pp. 62,63.

PART THREE

EVANGELIZING IN
THE ETHNIC MOSAIC

GETTING YOURSELF INVOLVED

Most Americans live within twenty miles of a non-Anglo ethnic, making a satisfying and fruitful outreach in the ethnic mosaic possible for each Christian. The Lord has brought these millions of people from all over the world into American neighborhoods, and each Christian in the United States needs to be moved with compassion to meet this great evangelistic need on his or her doorstep.

The ethnic peoples who enter the United States almost inevitably suffer from disorientation. American society contains much that is new and hard to understand, and a Christian's ethnic neighbors need someone to befriend them and to help them acclimate to this unfamiliar American culture. Any Christian in this nation can serve as a bridge to this new world, while at the same time sharing the love and the message of Jesus Christ.

A person who wishes to witness cross-culturally in America's ethnic communities must be sensitive and must want to develop a friendship. Any Christian who is willing to lay aside the comfort of his or her own kind and to minister to others in genuine love can participate in ethnic friendships and can become involved in sharing the gospel in multi-cultural America.

Everyone can initiate a friendship with an ethnic neighbor. A Christian family with children is just right for relating to many ethnic families. A couple, either young or old, can strike up a friendship with an immigrant family, while a single can help as a liaison for dealing with a newcomer's problems of integrating to a new language and culture. A senior citizen, being respected by the peoples of many cultures, has a distinct advantage in making friends with new arrivals and assisting them in their new environment.

Anyone can get involved in the challenging ministry of cross-cultural friendships and outreach to non-Anglos. Some suggestions are presented in this chapter to help the reader who is an Anglo-American Christian develop a personal strategy for reaching out to his or her ethnic neighbors.

INITIATE THE CONTACT

Once you are committed before God to befriending

ethnic people and to reaching them with the gospel, a contact with an international person or an ethnic family should be initiated. Finding people from other ethnic and cultural groups is easy. They can be met on university and college campuses, in businesses, at air terminals, through sponsorship, on the streets, in migrant camps, in local stores, and on your block.[1]

In initiating a contact with an international person or an ethnic family, prayer is vital.[2] Before beginning your cross-cultural friendship, you should ask the Lord to guide you to a person that you can learn to love. Pray for God to give you the courage to take the first step in starting the friendship. You should seek God's help in being a sensitive and loving friend and should also pray specifically for this new potential friend, asking God to help him to be open to your friendship.

If an international or an immigrant family lives in your neighborhood, you can go over to their home with some cookies, a loaf of bread, some flowers, or some fruit. While maintaining a friendly smile and a sincere manner, you may introduce yourself and present your gift. Without hidden motives, you should state your purpose – "I would like to be your friend."[3]

Since your small gift and your open manner should ease the fears of culture and language, you can relax and be yourself. A gesture of friendship with a smile and without pretense can overcome many barriers.[4] Language and cultural gaps can be bridged when friendliness and warmth are combined with genuine interest and patient understanding.

After slowly and carefully saying your name and introducing yourself, you can ask you ethnic neighbor his name. If he or she does not speak English, signs and words together can help. Care should be taken to pronounce the name respectfully, accurately, and carefully. Your attention to the correct pronunciation of his name will please him.

Since everyone loves the sound of his or her own name, you should avoid the temptation to give your ethnic neighbor an American nickname, unless he comes with one. Be sure to find out if a family name or first name is preferred, since the title used varies from culture to culture. In many countries it is a matter of courtesy and respect to address an individual by his or her proper name.[5]

After your brief greeting and introduction, make arrangements for a future visit. You can take out a pocket calendar and point to the date when you will return for another social call.[6] Once you have given him your name, address, and telephone number carefully printed on a card, then you may leave. You should make plans to go back a few days later to get to know your ethnic neighbor better. As an ambassador of God's love, you should take the initiative in the ethnic friendship and be willing to persevere in taking the lead in developing the relationship.

BUILD THE RELATIONSHIP

During future visits, you can become further acquainted with your ethnic neighbor. Since the presence of children often eliminates stiffness and tenseness, you should allow a preschooler to command the group's attention with a ball or an older child to share his favorite toy or his prized pet. Because older family members are frequently respected and revered in other cultures, older parents can easily begin a friendship with ethnic neighbors. If your ethnic friend is lonely for family and relatives in his home country, a child or an older parent serve as wonderful icebreakers and make your friend feel comfortable and relaxed.[7]

The conversation with your ethnic neighbor should always be kept positive, and this can be done by asking the proper questions. Your ethnic friend can often be drawn into a conversation by asking about his family, his impressions of American customs, his country, his language, his customs, and his religion. Differences in customs and culture frequently stimulate conversation.[8] You also should share about yourself, your family, and your background.

When your ethnic neighbor speaks little or no English, a small mail order catalog can be used as a picture book to draw him into conversation. You can ask him about his arrival in America and the country from which he came, employing a world map to trace the routes of his journeys and the locations of his friends and relatives. A small photo album of your family and the places where you have lived can be shared with him, and you can make use of pens and paper for drawing pictures of what you lack words for.

If you take along a book of words and sentences in your two languages, the two of you can take turns learning bits of each other's language, such as counting to ten or saying a common greeting. Interest and conversation can be sparked with recordings of music or with home

131

slides or movies. Nonverbal games, such as puzzles or dominoes, or hand craft material, such as play dough, provide entertainment for adults and children alike. The sharing of a hobby or project, such as embroidery, carving, or stamp-collecting, encourages a more informal atmosphere and provides something specific about which to talk.[9]

SERVE THE NEEDS

As your friendship with your ethnic neighbor is established, you can look for ways to serve your friend. Being sensitive to his physical needs is one way to minister to your neighbor. Basic necessities, such as lamps, bedding, chairs, table, dishes, and the like are immediate needs for any newly arriving family. You and your Christian friends may find some of these articles in your attic, basement, or garage or in a second-hand store. Proper seasonal clothing and shoes may be needed for the family members, and Christian friends or local merchants can often provide these items free or at a reduced price.

Another way to serve the needs of your ethnic friend is to assist him with needed community service information. If your friend is a newcomer to this country, he may need help in finding adequate housing for his family or in enrolling his children in school. You can help him to find doctors and dentists, to locate the post office, to discover the best buys in groceries and the place to purchase his ethnic food, to fill out applications and forms, to use public transportation, or to buy and service a car. Likewise, an explanation of the money system or a visit to the bank can greatly aid your ethnic neighbor's adjustment to this new country.

Assisting your friend in acquiring English skills is an additional way in which you can serve his needs. Formal language instruction may be necessary, and you can help enroll your friend and his family in English classes in the community and encourage continuing language training. Of course, by using lessons books, language guides, or picture books, you too can help him learn conversational English.[10]

ENRICH THE FRIENDSHIP

As you continue to enrich your relationship with your ethnic neighbor, you can look for ways to love him. You should be praying specifically for the international or ethnic family with whom you are visiting. Love, sensitivity, and patience will be important, and observing without judging and being very slow to criticize will be key. While it is not always easy to understand your friend whose culture is different, acceptance and love of your ethnic neighbor is possible.

Being a good listener and observer also opens the way for a deeper, richer friendship. You should resist the common tendency to do all of the talking and should listen attentively to those things which are important to your friend. When you do speak, you should avoid idioms and slang and speak slowly and distinctly, looking for signs of faulty communication and misunderstanding. Moreover, learning a few words in his language will give you a chance to empathize with your friend's struggle to master English and will allow him to have some laughs at your expense as you struggle to trill an "r" or nasalize an "ng."

Likewise, a cross-cultural friendship is enriched by being a learner. The ethnic person will be flattered when you want to know about his lifestyle, customs, food, clothing, and ideas and will communicate most fluently and comfortably when you are allowing him to converse about familiar things. Reading about his country in an encyclopedia, following his country in the news, and accompanying him to cultural events will demonstrate your respect for his cultural background. Your friendship will be further enriched by sending your ethnic neighbor birthday cards, notes, and letters, by engaging in activities which he enjoys, and by spending time together.[11]

OPEN YOUR LIFE AND HOME

In the context of your developing friendship, you should open up your life and home to allow your ethnic friend to observe you. Your ethnic neighbor can be invited to weddings, graduations, tours, weekend trips, holiday celebrations, picnics, and meals in your home. Often a written invitation, followed by a telephone call, can help your friend understand the event and can avoid any misunderstanding about dress, the beginning and ending times, and whether the activity includes a meal.

Sharing a relaxed, unhurried meal is a time honored

way for people to open their lives and homes to others. In most cultures, hospitality is an important way to nurture friendships. When inviting your ethnic neighbor for a meal, you should remember that an informal visit and meal together is better than an elaborate dinner or a situation with unfamiliar customs. A simple meal is easy for you to prepare and serve and easy for your friend who is trying to learn American customs. Moreover, an informal meal leaves open the possibility that your ethnic friend can return the favor and live up to your expectations.

In advance of his visit, you should learn of any dietary restrictions that your guest may have and should inquire about the foods he likes to eat at home so that you can safely use these in your meal preparation. The women in your ethnic friend's family should be allowed to participate in the kitchen, learning about American cooking and meal preparation. Your guest should also be informed about any cultural or family traditions, such as a prayer of thanks to God before the meal and what plate to use for rolls and which bowl for salad. Selecting an after dinner activity, like taking a ride to see downtown at night or attending a concert, will remove the pressure to talk if language is a difficulty.[12]

SHARE YOUR FAITH

In general, ethnic people in the United States are religious. While building the relationship, therefore, you should take advantage of any opportunity to give your ethnic friend New Testaments, tracts, and helpful gospel literature in their language.[13] A gift of the Scriptures in print can give you a natural opening for sharing the good news about Jesus.

Since your faith in God is an integral part of your life, you do not need to be afraid to share it when it comes up naturally in your conversations and relationships. By sharing a brief and clear personal testimony of what Jesus means to you in the experiences of daily life, you can demonstrate by your words the hope and meaning that Jesus brings to your life and can provide in the life of your ethnic neighbor. In a verbal witness to your international friend, however, keep the explanations of your faith in Christ simple, and be sensitive to the differences of language, culture, and religious background which will present unique needs and interests in the presentation of the gospel.

By inviting your ethnic friend to church, Bible study, or Vacation Bible School with you, you can give him an opportunity to learn English, as well as to meet other people who have a faith in Jesus Christ. Your ethnic neighbor should know exactly what to expect when he attends the church activity or service and should be made welcomed regardless of his religious background. The genuineness and openness of your witness and the faith of your Christian friends can do much to encourage your international friend in his spiritual pilgrimage.[14]

Opportunities for getting yourself involved in ministry to the ethnics in your community are nearly limitless. As you pray for your ethnic neighbors and cultivate their friendships, more and more openings will arise for you to share your faith and for God to work in their hearts to bring about the desired harvest. Several months, years, or generations may pass before results come, but your love, patience, and faithfulness may help many of your neighbors in America's ethnic mosaic to put their trust in the Lord Jesus Christ.

Endnotes

1. R. Max Kershaw, *How to Share the Good News with Your International Friend* (Colorado Springs, CO: International Students Incorporated, 1981), p. 3.

2. Lau, *The World at Your Doorstep*, p. 119.

3. Roy Weece, "The Strangers," *Christian Standard*, 11 March 1984, p. 19.

4. Raymond W. Hurn, *Guidelines for Launching Ethnic Congregations* (Kansas City, MO: Church Extension Ministries of the Church of the Nazarene, n.d.), p. 9.

5. Lau, *The World At Your Doorstep*, p. 120.

6. Lorna Anderson, *You and Your Refugee Neighbor* (Pasadena, CA: William Carey Library, 1980), pp. 13,14.

7. *An American Friend Handbook*, p. 6.

8. Karen Michener, "Unreached Among Us," *Moody*, March 1983, pp. 31,32.

9. Miriam Adeney, "Helping People Take Root," *The Mandate*, January 1985, pp. 1, 3.

10. See *An American Friend Handbook*, p. 29; Anderson, *You and Your Refugee Neighbor*, p. 16; Wallace W. Buckner, *Sponsors of Liberty Guide* (Atlanta, GA: Home Mission Board of the Southern Baptist Convention, 1986), pp. 14, 20,21; and Lewis, *Internationals*, pp. 12,13.

11. See *An American Friend Handbook*, pp. 4, 9,10, 12,16; Lau, *The World At Your Doorstep*, pp. 118-124; and Michener, "Unreached Among Us," pp. 31,32.

12. See *An American Friend Handbook*, pp. 2,3; Anderson, *You And Your Refugee Neighbor*, pp. 16,17; and Lau, *The World at Your Doorstep*, pp. 87,88, 119-121.

13. The American and Canadian Bible Societies publish Bibles and Scripture portions in most languages. Contact the American Bible Society, 1865 Broadway, New York, NY 10023, (212) 581-7400 or the Canadian Bible Society, 1835 Yonge Street, Toronto, ON M4S 1Y1, (419) 482-3081. The *New Life Testament* is an English translation using a vocabulary of only 850 words. Contract Christian Literature International, P.O. Box 777, Canby, OR 97013, (503) 266-9734.

14. See *An American Friend Handbook*, pp. 20-25; Michener, "Unreached Among Us," p. 32; Etheredge, *Migrants*, p. 10; and Lewis, *Internationals*, p. 16.

ENGAGING THE LOCAL CHURCH

No single, fail-safe way exists for a local church to engage in a cross-cultural ministry among those in the ethnic mosaic. Mobilizing the local church for ethnic evangelism can take many forms, but successful evangelism programs will require considerable preparation and planning. It must be remembered that a church is a moving, growing, and living organism which functions in the midst of neighborhoods and cities that change generationally, economically, culturally, and ethnically.

Any dynamic witness to ethnics will necessitate a constant attentiveness to and evaluation of the needs of those the Anglo-American church is seeking to reach with the gospel. A local church's effective involvement in evangelizing ethnics in the community will require that it be sensitive to the language and cultural differences, such as dress, style of worship, type of music, and the like. With this in mind, most any local church can utilize its in-house programs and local church people to engage in ministry to ethnic America.

A COMMITMENT TO PLANT CHURCHES

Engaging the local church in ethnic evangelism requires a commitment to planting churches. Planting new churches is an effective form of evangelism, and only recently have Anglo-American churches discovered the dynamic impact of ethnic church planting on reaching the mixture of ethnic groups in America and subsequently influencing the mission outreach of the church world-wide.[1]

The local church is the primary agent for any new church planting, and the Anglo-American church's basic commitment to new churches, especially new ethnic churches, is foundational to the evangelization of the United States. The time has come in the Anglo-American church for a renewed emphasis on investing in those efforts which lead to the establishment of new churches.

DEVELOP AWARENESS

Since many Anglo-Americans have very little appreciation for cultural differences, they do not know how to relate to people from other cultures, resulting in many lost opportunities for reaching the lost in ethnic America. Therefore, developing a corporate awareness of the multi-cultural fabric of this nation, encouraging a sensitivity toward people who are different, and creating a burden to reach non-Anglos with the gospel is essential for involving the local church in ethnic ministry.

Anglo-American Christians need to have a greater appreciation for cultural difference, an increased openness to another's point of view, and a deeper love for all people whom God has made in His image, regardless of background and nationality. Strong Biblical sermons on the equality of all men before God, lessons on world peoples, special racial and ethnic speakers, and films and books on ethnics and cultures can cultivate an awareness and sensitivity in the minds and hearts of Anglo-American Christians toward the many other ethnics in this nation who are different in appearance, speech, race, color, or social level. Joint worship services with non-English-speaking congregations, international meals, and ethnic cultural fairs can create understanding about America's pluralistic culture and can draw attention to the evangelistic need in the non-Anglo community.[2]

FIND OUT THE FACTS ABOUT THE TOTAL COMMUNITY

The local church that develops a corporate awareness of its Christian responsibility to share the gospel with ethnic neighbors should find out the facts about its total community. Most communities in America need some type of ethnic evangelism because non-Anglos are scattered everywhere throughout the country. Some ethnics will be quickly identifiable, while others will be discovered only after some research and careful observation.

By noticing ethnic restaurants, supermarkets, churches, clubs and organizations, and newspapers a local church can begin to locate the ethnic concentrations in its community. A visit to the census bureau or a local Chamber of Commerce can provide free material about who is living in the community and about the growth and migration trends in various ethnic neighborhoods.

Inquiries made at public libraries, public school districts offices, social welfare offices, and immigration offices can uncover much helpful information on the ethnicity of any community. Contacts made with the international student affairs departments of colleges and universities and with migrant and seasonal farm workers offices can uncover ethnics who reside nearby. A community survey may also be helpful in obtaining information which is available in no other way, such as the language spoken in the home, national background, religious preference, and church involvement and interest.[3]

A local Anglo-American church should find out what needs exist among the ethnics in its community and what resources are available to meet those needs by checking with mental health, social services, and other agencies. People will appreciate a sincere interest taken in them, and those ethnics with personal, social, and other needs will tend to be more receptive to the gospel message. An intensive look at the community will uncover a wealth of facts upon which a congregation can base a strategy of outreach.

PLAN AN OUTREACH STRATEGY

The information a local church gathers about its community will often reveal the need for evangelizing other ethnics nearby. If this is discovered, an Anglo-American congregation should not allow itself to be satisfied running the existing church programs. It, instead, needs to define an ethnic group to be reached and an approach to take, checking to see if any similar work is being attempted by other church groups.

The language spoken in the home, whether the people are first generation immigrants, their religious background, and their customs and habits will determine the local church's approach. Upon deciding whether to start the ethnic ministry in the local church or to launch a separate ethnic mission, definite plans need to be made to implement the congregation's strategy with the goal of meeting the needs of the ethnic people and of establishing an ethnic ministry which reflects the culture and language of the people.[4]

BUDGET THE FUNDS

The necessary funds for the ethnic outreach program need to be budgeted, and the resources for ethnic evangelism should be provided. A complete cost profile and analysis should include estimated costs for outreach projects, salaries for full-time or part-time workers, and costs for facilities. Expenses will be greatly reduced if the ethnic ministry shares the building with the sponsoring Anglo-American church, allowing more funds for paying the non-Anglo minister's salary.

Any new ethnic work will also require song books, Bibles, tracts, flyers, and signs in the ethnic language. In addition, assistance occasionally may be needed from the sponsoring congregation for printing, publicity, and mailings.[5] Local Anglo-American churches seriously concerned about the evangelization of ethnic America need to tithe and to do without some things because they choose to put their money into fulfilling the Great Commission in the non-Anglo segments of American society.

RECRUIT WORKERS

The local Anglo-American church needs to create a priority for the recruitment, training, and deployment of the necessary personnel for the task of ethnic evangelism. Leadership (both Anglo and non-Anglo) is needed to initiate, guide, plan, enlist, and train ethnic Christians for reaching their people. Such a leader needs to know the ethnic language, love the ethnic people, be spiritually mature, and have a compassion for the lost.[6] The right leadership is the secret to the success of any ethnic ministry.

The overseas church planting experience of mission personnel can be utilized to help win American ethnics. Bi-cultural ethnics who have an ability to relate transculturally can often mediate when tensions build up from misunderstandings with Anglos and non-Anglos.

Part-time, bi-vocational, or full-time ethnics who have a personal commitment to evangelism, church planting, and ministry among their own ethnic group are generally most successful in ethnic ministry leadership.[7]

Leaders from among the ethnic people should rise naturally to become Bible teachers, worship leaders, and elders as their personal lives warrant such ministry assignments. Such lay leaders, who speak the language, are acquainted with the culture, and are accepted readily by the ethnic people as leaders, minister best to the ethnic group.

PRAY

In establishing a witness and ministry among ethnics, it is important to acknowledge the priority of prayer and the guidance of the Holy Spirit in the process of planning.[8] Only God can prepare the way for visits with ethnics, and only His grace in the lives of those to be won will bring the fruit of true conversion.

A local Anglo-American church should form small prayer groups and plan specific prayer meetings to focus on the launching of its ethnic ministries. Prayer should be offered for mighty miracles to be performed among the lost and for God's kingdom to come in great power among the ethnics in its community. By uniting in prayer, by seeking His will, and by laboring for His glory, a mighty harvest can be reaped.

CULTIVATE ETHNIC CONTACTS

The local Anglo-American church will need to seek

out friendships with ethnics and show concern to them in active ways.[9] The key to building bridges of friendship is love and genuine interest in the individual. Any Anglo-American church or Christian can witness crossculturally to ethnics if he or she is sensitive, flexible, adaptable, sincere, and honest. Many ethnics will be receptive and appreciative of Christian friendships – especially those immigrants who are seeking social contacts or who need help with English or adjustment to their new country.

An excellent way for a church to respond to this opportunity to cultivate contacts with ethnics is by sponsoring an international student or refugee or by befriending an immigrant, diplomat, businessman, or migrant worker.[10] Through welcoming the newly-arriving ethnic at the airport, providing temporary housing, insuring that the children are enrolled in school instituting a job search, or providing friendship, the gospel message gains credibility and the ethnic neighbors receive a lasting positive impression in the name of Jesus.

These ethnic contacts will be enriched as the church prays for them, gets to know them, and becomes a sincere and friendly neighbor to them. An Anglo-American church can invite non-Anglos to special church services, Vacation Bible Schools, after school programs, international dinners, and recreational events where they can meet other Christians and become acquainted with others of their own nationality.[11] An active concern for newcomers displayed by the local Anglo-American church and a friendly involvement in their lives has contributed to the establishment of many ethnic ministries in the United States.

MEET NEEDS

Involving the local Anglo-American church in ethnic ministry should include meeting the physical, social, emotional, and economic needs of any ethnic contacts. This active concern will build tremendous bridges of love to ethnic neighbors which will earn the congregation the right to speak about the gospel and which will lend credibility to that message. Most ethnics will be reached with the gospel and gathered into functioning congregations only after Anglo-American Christians in local churches have demonstrated a concern for their needs and a sensitivity to their cultural forms.

This concern can be demonstrated in many ways. Some Christians can teach English, care for children, or lead vocational skills classes in sewing, typing, and other specialized subjects. Others can assist new immigrants by helping them obtain the legal, medical, domestic, or transportation counsel they need and by providing an orientation tour of the community. Some can help find housing, schedule job interviews, and enroll the children in school. Still others can provide basic clothing and household items for recent arrivals and their families.[12] In the midst of meeting these types of needs, opportunities will arise to share the gospel.

BEGIN THE ETHNIC MINISTRY

As contacts are cultivated and needs are met, a local

Anglo-American church can begin the ethnic ministry. At this strategic point of an ethnic's openness to the gospel, the local church needs effectively to evangelize its ethnic neighbors. This beginning point in the evangelistic ministry can take many different forms.

Often ethnic ministry begins within a church by sponsoring a non-Anglo individual or family.[13] The church members may want to host an ethnic family, inviting them to church services where a language translation could be available. A congregation may wish to offer a Bible school class in the ethnic language which meets at the same time as all other classes. A home fellowship of singing, preaching, Bible study, and social time could be held in the home of an ethnic contact for those who may not come to the church building. Church facilities could be made available for special ethnic interest groups or for language classes for those non-Anglos who want to learn English.

As the ethnic group grows, additional classes may be formed, an ethnic Bible School department may be developed, or worship services in the ethnic language may be initiated.[14] This ethnic mission within the Anglo-American church will share the facilities and will receive financial support from the church. This ethnic group may remain an organized unit within the church or may evolve into its own congregation over time. Regardless of the direction which the ethnic ministry takes within the church, it is essential that the ethnic mission have a voice in determining its leaders and programs and that the ethnic community view the Anglo-American congregation as wanting to serve the non-Anglo residents of the community.

At other times the ethnic ministry will begin by sponsoring and supporting a mission church in an ethnic community located in a different place from the sponsoring Anglo-American church.[15] In these situations the sponsoring church should share its resources and expertise with the ethnic ministry so that together the church of Christ might win more to the Lord. Since most ethnic congregations will be in urban settings, this partnership in ethnic church planting is a marvelous opportunity to enlist the participation of rural and suburban congregations in this great challenge of urban, ethnic church planting.

Any mission outreach to ethnic groups in another community should include Bible study and worship, should be guided by ethnic leaders whenever possible, should stress personal evangelism, and should maintain a style of worship and ministry which is sensitive to the differences in language and culture. Relationships with the sponsoring church should be defined carefully, help and training of ethnics by members of the sponsoring church should be encouraged, financial assistance should be decreased as responsibility by the ethnic congregation increases, and the progress of the ethnic congregation should be reviewed periodically by the sponsoring Anglo-American church. As the ethnic congregation moves toward maturity, it can become a fully self-supporting, self-sustaining, and self-propagating congregation.

EVALUATE THE WORK

Faithful attentiveness to the needs of the ethnic ministry and regular evaluation of the ethnic work is necessary to provide an effective witness in America's multi-cultural society. Appraisals of the outreach into the ethnic community need to be made, and adjustments that will strengthen the ethnic ministry need to be executed.

All regular reviews of the ethnic work by the local church, however, need to be done with a freedom from paternalistic control, with a sensitivity to the uniqueness of language and culture, and with a realization that the ethnic ministry may not proceed at the same pace or in the same way as the Anglo-American congregation is accustomed. Evaluations of the ethnic work should include input from the ethnic members of the ministry, and the local Anglo-American church, above all, should remain flexible.

Clearly, hundreds of local Anglo-American churches could engage in evangelistic outreach to the ethnic mosiac in the United States, many without buying property or investing large amounts of money. Opportunities for ethnic ministry by many congregations is limited only by vision, creativity, and available contacts.

A small, yet fast-growing, number of local Anglo-American churches have discovered the mission field in this multi-cultural nation and have initiated evangelistic ministries especially designed to reach their ethnic neighbors nearby. These ministries have not been launched without a struggle, but they are growing and producing fruit. More local Anglo-American churches need to join their ranks and vigorously become involved in efforts at cross-cultural ethnic ministries in towns and cities across the country.

Endnotes

1. Roger Boatman, "The Mission Field Has Come Home," p. 7.

2. See Duren and Wilson, *The Stranger Who Is Among You,* pp. 30-32 and Wallace W. Buckner, *How To Celebrate Language Missions Day,* Atlanta, GA, 1986. (Pamphlet.)

3. See Duren and Wilson, *The Stranger Who Is Among You,* pp. 32,33 and Hurn, *Guidelines For Launching Ethnic Congregations,* pp. 3,4.

4. *Guide For Establishing Ethnic Ministries and Congregations* (Atlanta, GA: Home Mission Board of the Southern Baptist Convention, 1986), p. 3.

5. Francisco G. Barajas, "Ethnic Evangelism In The USA," workshop given at the North American Christian Convention, Indianapolis, IN, 9 July 1986. (Printed.)

6. Leobardo C. Estrada, Sr., "How To Work With Different Language Groups," in *How To Start New Mission/Churches: A Guide For Associational Mission Leaders,* eds. J.V. Thomas and Carl A. Elder (Dallas, TX: Baptist General Convention Of Texas, 1979), pp. 64-67.

7. See Don Byers, "Looking At A Mosaic," *All The People,* n.d., p.3. and Home Mission Board of the Southern Baptist Convention, *Ethnic Missions Director,* Atlanta, GA, 1989, pp. 2,3. (Pamphlet.)

8. Hurn, *Guidelines For Launching Ethnic Congregations,* pp. 7,8.

9. The suggestions in Chapter 9, "Getting Yourself Involved," are also applicable to churches wishing to cultivate ethnic contacts.

10. The types of ethnics which may be located in a local church's community are discussed in Chapter 3, "The Diversity In Ethnic America," and in Chapter 4, "The Make-Up Of The Ethnic Mosaic."

11. See Hurn, *Guidlines for Launching Ethnic Congregations,* pp. 9-11; *Guide for Establishing Ethnic Ministries And Congregations,* pp. 3,4; and J.V. Thomas, "How To Relate To The Resources Of The Baptist General Convention Of Texas," in *How To Start New Mission/Churches: A Guide For Associational Mission Leaders,* eds. J.V. Thomas and Carl A. Elder (Dallas, TX: Baptist General Convention of Texas, 1979), p. 36.

12. See Buckner, *Sponsors Of Liberty,* pp. 8, 14-22; Lewis, *Internationals,* pp. 12-15; and Duren and Wilson, *The Stranger Who Is Among You,* pp. 33-37.

13. *Sponsors of Liberty,* p. 23.

14. *Guide For Establishing Ethnic Ministries And Congregations,* pp. 4,5.

15. Roberto Garcia, "How To Lead Churches To Develop Cross-Cultural Mission Units," in *How To Start New Missions/-Churches: A Guide For Associational Mission Leaders,* eds. J.V. Thomas and Carl A. Elder (Dallas, TX: Baptist General Convention of Texas, 1979), pp. 48-51.

PATTERNS IN ETHNIC MINISTRY

The ethnic peoples, who have undertaken the painfully slow process of adaptation to the mainstream of American society, are caught between two cultures. Their loyalty is divided between their native country and their newly adopted homeland, and they look for ways to understand and orient themselves to their new lives.

The patterns of pluralism and assimilation among ethnic groups are many and varied. The diversity in the styles of the many different ethnic backgrounds and responses intensifies the complexity of the ministry of the church in the ethnic mosaic. While the Anglo-American church can provide the bridge between these two worlds as it reaches out with the gospel of Jesus Christ in genuine love, it will need to learn to diversify its ministry in order to reach and hold the many types of ethnic peoples in this pluralistic nation.

PATTERNS IN ACCULTURATION

As the Anglo-American church bridges the gap with the gospel, Anglo-American Christians need to recognize that the different patterns of acculturation, or adaptation, for these ethnic peoples in America will require different kinds of evangelistic Bible studies and churches. It is impossible to think of all the people in a particular ethnic group as being all alike. Changes in ethnic values, customs, language, social networks, and cultural forms within the overall framework of the dominant Anglo-American experience produce a dilemma for each individual ethnic.

The tug between assimilation into the Anglo-American mold and attachment to his distinctive ethnic heritage creates pressure for each person in the non-Anglo community as he wrestles with his ethnic identity. Each individual has many ways to deal with his baffling ethnic distinctiveness in this new environment.[1]

For instance, the recently arrived immigrant brings with him his home culture, speaks only his native language, lives in his own cultural groups as much as possible, maintains his ethnic traditions, and feels terribly insecure in his new surroundings. His identity is drawn completely from his ethnic heritage and values, making his ethnic identity the controlling factor in most areas of his life.[2] As a result, very little integration takes place, and a church or a Bible study in his native language will be needed to reach him with the gospel.

Another immigrant who has lived in America for a few years would be able to speak some English, relate somewhat to the Anglo-American life around him, and be secure enough to venture often outside the confines of his ethnic group. He has mingled the two cultures, but he may not understand American cultural nuances. Although he may refer to his country of origin as "home," his ethnic heritage is not absolutely essential to his self-conscious identity.[3] This ethnic might be reached with either an ethnic or a bi-lingual church or Bible study.

A third immigrant could be almost entirely English, speaking and integrated into the cultural patterns and lifestyle of America. This ethnic would have difficulty relating to a recently arrived immigrant, even though he is not fully at home in Anglo-American society. He may identify with his ethnic group when it is convenient and beneficial, but his knowledge of the ethnic language and his loyalty to his ethnic past is limited.[4] An Anglo-American church with an ethnically sensitive style or a bi-cultural ethnic church or Bible study could reach him.

A fourth immigrant could have been in America for some time, have rejected his ethnic values and heritage, and have adapted to his new identity as an American. This ethnic has a disdain for anything that is not totally American and preserves no relationship with his ethnic language.[5] He will only be reached with an Anglo-American church or Bible study.

A fifth immigrant could be the child or grandchild of an immigrant, be bi-lingual and bi-cultural, and have a degree of uneasiness with complete orientation to Anglo-American traditions, but have difficulty identifying entirely with the cultural patterns of his ancestors. He accepts the best of both cultures, retains some identity with both, has the capacity to live in both worlds simultaneously, and possesses a pride for his unique bi-cultural heritage.[6] He will need to be reached by a church or Bible study group that understands and affirms bi-cultural patterns.

Various degrees of cultural integration or mixing exist among ethnic groups. Different ethnic groups move through these patterns of acculturation in different periods of time – some in a lifetime and others over many generations. As outsiders, the Christians in the Anglo-American church need to see the spectrum of various levels of assimilation for ethnic immigrants and to recognize the various challenges for the presentation of the gospel to each type of immigrant in transition. The Anglo church in America must accept the responsibility of reaching these ethnic immigrants with the gospel of Jesus Christ and of presenting the gospel in a manner that will be received and accepted by them at their level of cultural adaptation.

PATTERNS OF CHURCHES

Many ethnics in America are most responsive to the

gospel when approached in a manner that is sensitive to language and cultural differences; therefore, any outreach into this multi-cultural nation should be careful not to force assimilation on the ethnic group. The differences in culture, language, and patterns of acculturation make it necessary for care to be taken in any attempts to evangelize America's diverse ethnic population.

The type of church or Bible study needed to reach non-Anglos will depend on many factors, though most of these ethnics are not going to be won into typical Anglo-American congregations. Anglo-American Christians should not expect that non-Anglos will eventually become like them and assimilate into their churches. Acculturation to Anglo-American Christianity may never occur for many ethnic peoples, nor is it desirable for some.

Most ethnics will look for a Christian group that affirms their ethnicity and gives them the chance to worship in a language and culture with which they are most comfortable and familiar. They will largely need to be won into ethnic congregations and Bible study groups. This means the multiplying of different kinds of ethnic churches and Bible studies in ethnic communities all across the country.

One type of ethnic outreach is the sponsoring and supporting of a separate mono-ethnic church in an ethnic community located in a separate place from the sponsoring Anglo-American church.[7] This outreach mission may be in a home, a church facility, or a rented building. Although a mono-ethnic congregation in a separate location would tend to be more expensive and could be deficient in the necessary programs for meeting the needs of the second generation ethnic, it would provide the optimum social cohesion for the ethnic group and would encourage indigeneity.

A second type of ethnic outreach is a separate mono-ethnic church in the same location as an Anglo-American congregation. In this pattern of multi-ethnic ministry an Anglo congregation deliberately plans for and introduces an ethnic group into its facility on a permanent basis, or a waning congregation in the midst of an ethnically changing neighborhood adjusts to meet the needs of the incoming ethnic group.

Since the individual needs of each group are met through the two distinct congregations which satisfy the language and cultural needs of all, the separate mono-ethnic churches do not share a sense of unity in their ministry. Nevertheless, if harmony and love are maintained between the groups, two independent mono-ethnic churches can meet in the same building, can be united in Christ, and can impact the two ethnic communities with the gospel.[8]

A third type of ethnic outreach is a mono-ethnic Bible study group, prayer cell, or Bible school unit among the ethnic community which meets in the Anglo-American church building. This efficient sharing of the church facilities not only allows for ethnic distinctiveness within the Anglo-American congregation but also permits the integration of the youth and children's programs and encourages the social interaction of the various ethnic groups.[9] The ethnic group may remain an organized unit within the church or may evolve into its own congregation over time.

Fig. 7. Patterns of Churches

1. Separate mono-ethnic church in separate place

2. Separate mono-ethnic church in same location

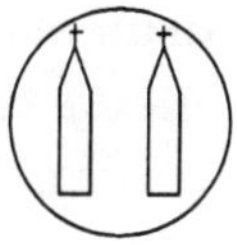

3. Mono-ethnic unit in the Anglo congregation

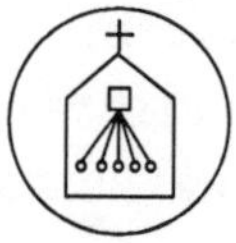

4. Multi-ethnic, semi-autonomous congregations

5. One church assimilating all

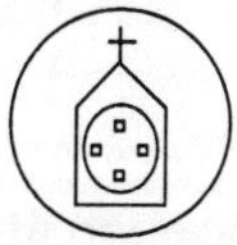

A fourth type of ethnic outreach is multi-ethnic, semi-autonomous congregations within the church. Separate language services are conducted simultaneously in different parts of the building, programs and personnel are shared and integrated in every way, and unity of doctrine and goals exists. Although leadership and decision making for this one church is complex, the congregation has the resources to meet the variety of needs in the multi-ethnic community.[10]

A final type of ethnic outreach is one church that assimilates all ethnic groups who come. The members of more than one ethnic group meet together and form one tightly knit group, experiencing the oneness of genuine Christian community. Even though this congregation will not reach those people who are unable to relate to the amalgamated culture or the common language, her ministry can build bridges of understanding and relationships between various ethnic groups.[11]

Because many factors contribute to the ethnic distinctiveness of America's immigrants, different patterns exist for organizing ethnic ministry. No single evangelistic response is sufficient to effectively share the gospel message in ethnic America. Various patterns of mono-ethnic, as well as multi-ethnic, types of outreach are important for reaching those ethnic people in different stages of acculturation who do not relate completely to Anglo-American culture nor share exclusively the English language.

In many communities in America another kind of church or Bible study is needed to reach ethnic immigrants with the gospel. Every Anglo-American church in every location should be open and flexible in its evangelism and outreach, using whatever pattern of ministry that will bring people in the ethnic mosaic to the Lord and into His Kingdom.

Endnotes

1. Abramson, "Assimilation and Pluralism," pp. 150-160.

2. Duren and Wilson, *The Stranger Who Is Among You*, pp. 16-18.

3. Charles L. Chaney, *Church Planting At The End Of The Twentieth Century* (Wheaton, IL: Tyndale House, 1984), pp. 162,163.

4. Richard W. Colenso, "Evangelism Among Ethnic Peoples In The United States," paper presented at the Consultation on Contemporary Evangelism of the National Association of Evangelicals, Des Plaines, IL, 29-30 November 1976, pp. 3,4.

5. Knight, "Ministering With European Language Groups," p. 56.

6. Oscar Romo, "Discovering The American Ethnic," *The Mandate*, March 1985, pp. 3,4.

7. Hurn, *Guidelines For Launching Ethnic Congregations*, pp. 12,13.

8. Montoya, *Hispanic Ministry In North America*, pp. 69,70.

9. *Guide For Establishing Ethnic Ministries And Congregation*, pp. 4,5.

10. Wagner, *Our Kind Of People*, pp. 159,160.

11. Duren and Wilson, *The Stranger Who Is Among You*, pp. 39-42.

12

THE INDISPENSABILITY
OF ETHNIC CHURCH PLANTING

The Anglo-American churches which will grow during the next decade will probably be those that are convinced of the indispensability of ethnic church planting and are committed to the multiplication of ethnic churches in the United States as their highest evangelistic priority. The growing cross-cultural mission challenge in America can be met only by motivating Anglo and non-Anglo Christians for cross-cultural evangelism and church planting in the ethnic mosaic.

This launching of ethnic and non-English language churches across the United States is urgent and necessary if millions of people within America's borders are going to be reached with the gospel. Far too many non-Anglo peoples in this nation are insulated from hearing

163

the gospel because of language or culture.

Initiating evangelistic programs, planting churches, and maintaining ethnic ministries which target these unchurched segments among the non-Anglo population is essential for meeting the spiritual needs of those in ethnic America. Supporting church planting as an indispensable priority and keeping it vigorous and thriving among America's ethnic population will necessitate a commitment to the importance of churches planting churches, to the development of indigenous leadership and leadership training, to the mobilization of cross-cultural workers, and to the preparation of ethnic and non-English language literature.

CHURCHES PLANTING CHURCHES

Sheer numbers of ethnic immigrants abundantly prove that there exists a need for multitudes of new churches among America's ethnic communities. No more effective method of evangelizing this multi-ethnic nation exists than the involvement of Anglo-American churches in the planting of non-Anglo churches.

Since the responsibility for evangelizing America's population rests primarily with the local churches, Anglo and non-Anglo congregations that are not actively involved in evangelism and church planting among ethnics need to catch a vision for reaching ethnic America for Christ through the starting of ethnic and non-English language congregations. Planting multi-ethnic congregations will allow the existing church buildings to be used by more than one language group, while planting mono-ethnic congregations in a particular ethnic community where no church exists will stimulate the ethnic believers in their vision for the evangelization of ethnic America.

Without abandoning existing programs, thousands of local Anglo churches in America can actively begin churches among newly arriving immigrants. No more opportune time exists to share the gospel and to begin ethnic churches than as recent arrivals seek social contacts with others from their home country and desire help with starting their new lives in America.

Churches in America that plant ethnic churches will be intensely evangelistic, expecting everyone to spread the gospel to all peoples.[1] Local membership, as well as ethnic contacts, will be mobilized in the proclamation of the gospel at school, at the office, in the restaurant, in the market, and on the playground to people who are not of their particular culture or language.

Since ethnics will be most successful in bringing their own people to salvation, non-Anglo Christians need to be given the freedom and support by Anglo-Christians to evangelize their own people. Ethnic Christians are the most effective evangelists for reaching their own people with the gospel.[2] Evangelism in ethnic America, therefore, need not be done merely by Anglo-Americans nor in the Anglo-American way alone.

Because most of the ethnic immigrants are going to need to be won into congregations that are overwhelmingly ethnic in culture, language, dress, eating habits, marriage patterns, music, and worship styles, giving up ethnic distinctives in order to take on Anglo-American forms should not be a requirement in ethnic church planting. Anglo-American churches need to be willing to modify church traditions and methods to fit the ethnic culture in which they are attempting to work. Churches that ignore the ethnic differences or refuse to allow non-Anglos the space to develop their own styles of ministry will fail in ethnic church planting.[3]

A growing concern and involvement in those mission efforts which leads to the starting of new ethnic churches will profoundly impact the growth of the American church and its influence in the evangelization of the world. As money, talents, and people are invested in missions which evangelistically reach out beyond the Anglo-American population to the lost in the other ethnic groups of this nation, a commitment to the indispensability of churches planting ethnic churches will be established as a top priority for Anglo-American Christians.

INDIGENOUS LEADERSHIP AND LEADERSHIP TRAINING

The development of indigenous leadership and leadership training is essential for successfully keeping the momentum of ethnic church planting going. A clear correlation exists between the number of new ethnic churches and the availability of indigenous leaders. Churches which lack ethnic leaders or a means for training ethnic leaders are not able to effectively and rapidly start churches among new ethnic groups.[4]

Prepared indigenous leadership is one of the most important elements in planting an ethnic church and maintaining the growth of that congregation. Ethnic leadership can be developed with both formal and informal training, as well as with the use of ethnic leaders from overseas churches.

Formal training may include traditional seminary preparation, as well as certificate programs at college and seminary extensions. It should be noted, however, that the educational background of some ethnic groups and their view of leadership make the long, expensive, and tedious academic requirements of seminary training irrelevant and impractical in many ethnic church planting situations. Moreover, many young ethnics who go away from their own culture for four to seven years to receive their college or seminary training become alienated from their own people and culture and are unable or unwilling to return to their ethnic communities at the end of their educational preparation.

Functional, local church oriented training, therefore, is what is often needed. New, innovative programs of training for ethnic leaders, which emphasize the basics, keep the student in close contact with the local church, and prepare him for nurturing the church, need to be developed by colleges and seminaries. If formal training programs are flexible, affordable, accessible to the ethnic leaders, and culturally relevant, they can adequately prepare indigenous ethnic leaders for the rapidly growing needs of ethnic churches.[5]

Informal training can also train ethnic workers for leadership. This preparation should produce leaders who can effectively evangelize their people, guide the local church worship and growth, and train others to carry on the work of ministry. Since most ethnic churches honor age, maturity, and proven ministry effectiveness as requirements for assuming leadership, successful ministry in ethnic America is not so related to formal seminary training as to living out Christ's life in the daily context of life.[6] This makes informal education of ethnic workers an effective alternative to the preparation of indigenous leadership.

Many ethnic leaders who are bi-vocational and who cannot quit their jobs and move their families to an educational training facility can be prepared through informal on-the-job training weekly or bi-weekly class sessions which include Bible study, sermon preparation, evangelism, discipling, and counseling. Many of these leaders work by day and minister by night and on weekends and can receive the clear Biblical teaching and practical ministry preparation that they need through such informal training. Likewise, the Anglo-American church should not overlook the large pool of leaders from overseas churches whose experience and expertise can be utilized in the evangelization of ethnic America. The mobile world of today makes it possible for these Christian leaders to migrate to the ethnic churches of the United States so that they can evangelize people from their culture, language, and background who are now living in America.[7]

CROSS-CULTURAL WORKERS

Many kinds of workers, besides indigenous leaders, need to be mobilized to carry out the task of planting ethnic churches. Because the ethnic speaks another language and comes from a different cultural heritage, Anglo-American workers need to be prepared for cross-cultural ministry in the United States. Anglo-American churches need to prayerfully commission these workers for special ethnic ministry.

With the clear difference between home and foreign missions gradually fading, the overseas church planting experience of mission personnel are an exciting resource that can be utilized to help win non-Anglos and to plant ethnic congregations in this nation. Seasoned missionaries who have retired or who for various reasons may not be able to return to the foreign field are uniquely prepared by years of labor in the language and culture of a particular people and can effectively minister to that people group in America's multi-cultural society.[8]

Mission recruits can also be mobilized as cross-cultural workers for reaching the myriad of ethnic groups in this country. They can receive training in America's multi-cultural setting that will better equip them for the mission field. A one-year or two-year internship in an ethnic church planting ministry among the population from the countries where the recruit hopes to work will provide him with an introduction to the culture and language, with a network of personal relationships among the people, and with the practical preparation in cross-cultural ministry that will equip him to be a successful missionary overseas.[9]

Cross-cultural workers, likewise, can be mobilized for the planting of ethnic churches through the formation of church planting teams. Individuals of all ages and any marital status could commit themselves for two years to begin a church within a targeted ethnic group. Whether supported by others or self-supporting, each team member could dedicate at least fifteen hours each week to evangelism, discipleship, and nurturing in the ethnic community. Upon the establishment of the ethnic congregation, the team members could move on or remain as permanent members of the ethnic church.[10]

Although overseas missionaries, mission recruits, and church planting teams can be mobilized to plant ethnic churches, Anglo-American churches, colleges, and seminaries in the United States should initiate programs to alert and prepare all Christian workers to evangelize cross-culturally in the United States. Cross-cultural ability and education is no longer a luxury but a necessity for Christian workers. The acquisition of a second language is increasingly more important in equipping these workers to minister in America's multicultural society.

Today's church leaders need cross-cultural training and background to be equipped to communicate across cultural barriers and to meet the challenge of ethnic evangelism. Anglo-American churches and training institutions should encourage this kind of bi-lingual and bi-cultural preparation for all present and future leadership.[11]

ETHNIC AND LANGUAGE LITERATURE

The preparation of ethnic and non-English language literature is crucial to maintaining the momentum in ethnic ministries and to supporting church planting as an indispensable priority. The Anglo-American church needs to create sound cross-cultural presentations of the gospel which recognize the wide variety of cultural, religious, linguistic, and educational factors involved in sharing the gospel with non-Anglos.

The gospel message has to be woven into the fabric of a group's ethnic heritage, communicated in a language that is clear and culturally relevant, and taught in a manner that captures the attention of the ethnic learner and brings him to an understanding of Biblical truth and obedience to that truth. The availability of adequate materials with sensitive and simple explanations of the gospel will often determine the effectiveness and the fruitfulness of church planting in ethnic communities.[12]

The priority of ethnic church planting is indispensable if the Anglo-American church is to maintain an outreach to ethnic America. The urgency of reaching the huge numbers of ethnics in this nation demands that churches in the United States become committed to the importance of churches planting churches, to the development of indigenous leadership and leadership training, to the mobilization of cross-cultural workers, and to the preparation of ethnic and language materials. Ethnic church planting which emphasizes these significant elements for effective ethnic ministry will generate life, vitality, and excitement in the evangelization of the ethnic mosaic in North America and will maintain an outreach to the millions of people within this nation's borders who need to hear the gospel.

171

Endnotes

1. Montoya, *Hispanic Ministry In North America*, pp. 49-51, 148-150.

2. See Duren and Wilson, *The Stranger Who Is Among You*, p. 34 and Oscar Romo, "Planting Ethnic Churches," *MissionsUSA*, November-December 1989, p. 37.

3. M. Wendell Belew, "Conclusion," in *Missions In The Mosaic*, comp. M. Wendell Belew (Atlanta, GA: Home Mission Board of the Southern Baptist Convention, 1974), p. 86; *Guide For Establishing Ethnic Ministries And Congregations*, p. 1; and Roger S. Greenway, "The Ends Of The Earth Have Come To Town," in *Cities: Mission's New Frontier*, Roger S. Greenway and Timothy M. Monsma (Grand Rapids, MI: Baker Book House, 1989), pp. 66,67.

4. See W. Dayton Roberts, "Theological Education, Church Planting, Go Hand-In-Hand," *The Mandate*, October 1985, p. 10 and Home Mission Board, "Language Missions Facts," p. 14.

5. See Home Mission Board of the Southern Baptist Convention *Language Missions Concepts: Ethnic Leadership Development*, Atlanta, GA, 1987, (Pamphlet.), and Duren and Wilson, *"The Stranger Who Is Among You"*, pp. 55-58.

6. Roger A. Greenway, "Goals of Urban Ethnic Evangelism," in *Cities: Mission's New Frontier*, Roger S. Greenway and Timothy M. Monsma (Grand Rapids, MI: Baker Book House, 1989). pp. 88,89.

7. Jerry Appleby, "The Global Significance Of Reaching Ethnics In The United States," *The Mandate*, October 1985, p. 15.

8. Art McCleary, "Mission Opportunities At Your Doorstep," *Mission Frontiers*, November-December 1989, p. 22.

9. Greenway, "The Ends Of The Earth Have Come To Town," p. 69.

10. Duren and Wilson, *The Stranger Who Is Among You*, pp. 52-54.

11. Greenway, *"The Shift To Ethnic Mission,"* p. 1.

12. Home Mission Board, *Language Missions Facts*, p. 14.
172

CONCLUSION

"Red and yellow, black and white" – ethnic peoples of every hue and from every shore are coming to America and are residing in American communities. At the end of the Twentieth Century, God in His own way has brought the world to America and has made it possible for virtually every Christian in the United States to actually impact the world for Christ. There are no visas, no government restrictions, and total religious freedom. For each American Christian, the diversity of this multi-cultural nation is undeniable and the need to reach out in ethnic evangelism is urgent.

God has called His church to evangelize this multi-ethnic America. However, although the Lord has allowed unreached peoples of the world to come to this nation in unprecedented numbers, they remain nearly as unevangelized in the United States as they were in their native countries. Estimates indicate that less than one-half of one percent of all ethnics are being reached by the gospel witness of Anglo-American churches.

Truly the church in America today must regard itself as being in a missionary situation. The number of unchurched ethnics in the country make America one of the larger mission fields needing the gospel, and these unreached segments of American society can be identified by language, culture, and geography. Many of these lost stand in the shadow of a sleeping Anglo-American church, unaware of the spiritual needs of those in its community. The Anglo-American church must deliberately and soon rise to this tremendous opportunity and challenge for reaching these unevangelized ethnic neighbors for Christ.

Nevertheless, it is often easier for Anglo-American Christians to be kept from sharing the gospel with the multitude of ethnic groups on their doorsteps because of indifference, fears, and provincialism. They frequently retreat to the comfort and security of their own kind in their Anglo-American Christian community rather than reach out to those who may be different in color, language, and culture.

When far away in their home nations, these various ethnic peoples receive the Anglo-American church's interest, missionary monies, and personnel. But, when non-Anglos are close by, they threaten the Anglo-American church, and Anglo-American Christians often withdraw or flee without a deliberate effort to reach them with the gospel. Anglo-American Christians, however, cannot wait until these ethnic peoples become Anglicized before they evangelize them. The time to reach these millions in multi-cultural America is now!

Today's Anglo-American church is faced with this significant evangelistic opportunity and comes perilously close to squandering it. Twenty-five years ago, when the immigration laws of the United States were relaxed to let in many foreigners, the church in America was not prepared to minister to these ethnic peoples. Twenty-five years later, Anglo-American Christians still struggle with facing this enormous evangelistic challenge.

Anglo-American congregations must respond positively to this mission opportunity, must develop God's love and compassion for all peoples, and must reach out with the redeeming love of Jesus Christ to the non-Anglos in their communities before it is too late. The Anglo Christians in the United States need to become committed to active outreach among the "Red and yellow, black and white" ethnics in America, not simply to a sympathetic tolerance of ethnic and minority participation in their congregations. Winning America demands winning the people in America's ethnic mosaic. The Anglo-American church must become a missionary church.

The ethnic presence will remain a permanent fixture of American life. To a large extent the growing churches of the next decade will be those communities of believers who have faced the ethnic challenge, have implemented ethnic outreach, have established multi-cultural and multi-ethnic ministries, and have recognized and accepted all peoples, regardless of ethnic background.

Today, by using existing facilities, hundreds of congregations across America could start an ethnic church without buying property. Many others could sponsor an outreach mission to an ethnic group in the United States. The Biblical responsibility to the lost dictates an urgency to demonstrate Christian concern for the unsaved among ethnic populations in this great nation and to establish multitudes of ethnic ministries across this land.

A small, yet fast-growing, number of Anglo-American churches have discovered this mission field nearby and have initiated cross-cultural ministries among the peoples in multi-ethnic America. These ethnic ministries have not been launched without a struggle, but they are growing and producing fruit. These efforts at cross-cultural ethnic ministries need to be multiplied in towns and cities across this country.

Since ethnics in America can be a bridge to the evangelization of the world, the church dare not shrink from this enormous opportunity. Anglo-American Christians must move into the unfamiliar terrain of reaching out with love and the gospel to the mission field among the ethnic groups in this country.

Although peoples from most of the mission fields of the world are living in America's multi-cultural society, the opportunities for sharing the gospel with them will not remain ripe forever. The time for the harvest of ethnic America is now!

Anglo-American Christians today should look around them at the needs of their ethnic neighbors, visualize what they can do to take the gospel to them, and pray for the Lord to use their lives in a mighty way as laborers in this vast harvest field. Anglo churches in America should start without delay to overcome the stumbling blocks of indifference, fears, and provincialism and to rise to the challenge of proclaiming a message of abundant life in Christ which many are waiting to hear. Anglo-American Christians should begin now to reach across cultural barriers to establish contact, provide loving friendship, and offer the message of salvation to the "red and yellow, black and white" in America's ethnic mosaic.

BIBLIOGRAPHY

Books

An American Friend Handbook. Colorado Springs, CO: International Students Incorporated, 1984.

Anderson, Lorna. *You and Your Refugee Neighbor.* Pasadena, CA: William Carey Library, 1980.

Balda, Wesley D., Ed. *Heirs of the Same Promise.* Arcadia, CA: National Convocation of Evangelizing Ethnic America, 1984.

Belew, M. Wendell, Comp. *Missions in the Mosaic.* Atlanta, GA: Home Mission Board of the Southern Baptist Convention, 1974.

Buckner, Wallace W. *Sponsors of Liberty Guide.* Atlanta, GA: Home Mission Board of the Southern Baptist Convention, 1986.

Chaney, Charles L. *Church Planting at the End of the Twentieth Century.* Wheaton, IL: Tyndale House, 1984.

Duran, James, and Wilson, Rod. *The Stranger Who Is Among You*. Pasadena, CA: William Carey Library, 1983.

Etheredge, Cecil D. *Ministry/Witness Resource Guide: Migrants*. Atlanta, GA: Home Mission Board of the Southern Baptist Convention, 1985.

Greenway, Roger S., and Monsma, Timothy M. *Cities: Mission's New Frontier*. Grand Rapids, MI: Baker Book House, 1989.

Guide for Establishing Ethnic Ministries and Congregations. Atlanta, GA: Home Mission Board of the Southern Baptist Convention, 1986.

Hurn, Raymond W. *Guidelines for Launching Ethnic Congregations*. Kansas City, MO: Church Extension Ministries of the Church of the Nazarene, n.d.

Kershaw, R. Max. *How To Share the Good News with Your International Friend*. Colorado Springs, CO: International Students Incorporated, 1981.

Lau, Lawson. *The World At Your Doorstep*. Downers Grove, IL: InterVarsity Press, 1984.

Lewis, James N. *Ministry/Witness Resource Guide: Internationals*. Atlanta, GA: Home Mission Board of the Southern Baptist Convention, 1987.

McGavran, Donald. *Understanding Church Growth*. Grand Rapids, MI: William B. Eerdmans Publishing Company, 1970.

Montoya, Alex D., *Hispanic Ministry in North America*. Grand Rapids, MI: Zondervan Publishing House, 1987.

Parvin, Earl. *MissionsUSA*. Chicago: Moody Press, 1985.

Thomas, J.V., and Elder, Carl A., Eds. *How to Start New Mission/Churches: A Guide for Associational Mission Leaders*. Dallas: Baptist General Convention of Texas, 1979.

Thornstrom, Stephen, Ed. *Harvard Encyclopedia of American Ethnic Groups*. Cambridge, MA: Harvard University Press, 1980.

Wagner, C. Peter. *Our Kind of People*. Atlanta, GA: John Knox Press, 1979.

Yamamori, Tetsunao. *God's New Envoys*. Portland, OR: Multnomah Press, 1987.

Newspapers

Eskey, Kenneth. "Hispanic Population Growing at Five Times Rest of U.S.". *New Hampshire Sunday News,* 15 October 1989, sec. B, p. 8.

Schmid, Randolph E. "U.S. Hispanic Population Continues Growth." *New Hampshire Sunday News,* 18 March 1990, sec. B, p. 4.

Pamphlets

Buchner, Wallace W. *How To Celebrate Language Missions Day.* Atlanta, GA: Home Mission Board of the Southern Baptist Convention, 1986. (Pamphlet.)

Home Mission Board of the Southern Baptist Convention. *Ethnic Missions Director.* Atlanta, GA: 1989. (Pamphlet.)

Home Mission Board of the Southern Baptist Convention. *Language Mission Concepts: Ethnic Leadership Development.* Atlanta, GA: 1987. (Pamphlet.)

Home Mission Board of the Southern Baptist Convention. *Language Missions Facts: 1988 Update.* Atlanta, GA: 1988. (Pamphlet.)

Home Mission Board of the Southern Baptist Convention. *We're Working with Europeans through Language Missions.* Atlanta. GA: 1986. (Pamphlet.)

Home Mission Board of the Southern Baptist Convention. *We're Working with Middle Easterners through Language Missions.* Atlanta, GA: 1986. (Pamphlet.)

Papers

Barajas, Francisco G. "Ethnic Evangelism in the USA." Workshop. North American Christian Convention. Indianapolis, IN: 9 July 1986. (Printed.)

Colenso, Richard W. "Evangelism Among Ethnic Peoples in the United States." Consultation on Contemporary Evangelism of the National Association of Evangelicals. Des Plaines, IL: 29-30 November 1976. (Mimeographed.)

International Missions. "Eastern Religions in North America." Wayne, NJ: n.d. (Mimeographed.)

Spicer, Jim. "What I Have Learned from Thirteen Years of Working in an Integrated Church and Neighborhood."

Workshop. North American Christian Convention. Indianapolis, IN: 8 July 1986. (Printed.)

Tingle, Donald S. "Islam Challenges the Church – What If the United States Became a Muslim Country?" Workshop. North American Christian Convention. Indianapolis, IN: 7 July 1986. (Printed.)

Wagner, C. Peter. "A Vision for Evangelizing the Real America." Plenary Session Address. National Convocation on Evangelizing Ethnic America. Houston, TX.: 15 April 1985. (Printed.)

Periodicals

Adeney, Miriam. "Helping People Take Root." *The Mandate.* January 1985, p. 1, 3.

Appleby, Jerry. "The Global Significance of Reaching Ethnics in the United States." *The Mandate.* October 1985, p. 15.

Boatman, Roger. "The Mission Field Has Come Home." *The Lookout.* 23 March 1980, pp. 6, 7, 11.

Broyles, Williams, Jr. "Promise of America." *U.S. News and World Report.* 7 July 1986, pp. 25-31.

Butterfield, Fox. "Why They Excel." *Parade Magazine.* 21 January 1990, pp. 4-6.

Byers, Don. "Looking at a Mosaic." *All the People.* n.d., p. 3.

Deuitch, Nelson L. "Toronto – The Meeting Place." *Christian Standard.* 28 January 1990, pp. 11-13.

"Go West, Go East." *U.S. News and World Report.* 7 July 1986. pp. 30,31.

Greenway, Roger S. "Reaching the Unreached in the Cities." *The Mandate.* October 1985, pp. 14,15.

Greenway, Roger S. "The Shift to Ethnic Mission." *The Mandate.* March 1985, p. 1.

Hullum, Everett. "The Internationals: The Diplomats." *MissionsUSA.* May-June 1987, pp. 5-17.

Kvaalen, Kristin. "Seamen's Mission: Gateway to the Unreached Peoples." *Mission Frontiers.* June – July 1989, pp. 4-7.

McCleary, Art. "Mission Opportunities at Your Doorstep." *Mission Frontiers.* November-December 1989, p. 22.

Michener, Karen. "Unreached Among Us." *Moody.* March

1983, pp. 31,32.

Netland, Harold. "Evangelical Theology of Mission and the Challenge of Pluralism." *Trinity World Forum.* Fall 1989, pp. 1-4.

Roberts, W. Dayton. "Theological Education, Church Planting, Go Hand-in-Hand." *The Mandate.* October 1985, p. 10.

Romo, Oscar. "Discovering the American Ethnic." *The Mandate.* March 1985, pp. 3,4.

Romo, Oscar. "Planting Ethnic Churches." *MissionsUSA.* November-December 1989, p. 37.

Romo, Oscar. "The Asian Challenge." *MissionsUSA.* January-February 1990, pp. 44,45.

Romo, Oscar. "Twentieth-Century Sojourners." *Missions-USA.* January-February 1987. p. 33.

Spring, Beth. "Refugees: Off Sinking Boats into American Churches." *Christianity Today.* 15 June 1984, pp. 26-29.

"The Newest Markets for New Churches." *Visionary.* June 1989, p. 3.

Tingle, Don. "Over Here." *Asian Evangelism.* October-December 1987, pp. 1,3.

Tutterow, Michael. "More Evangelical Attention Needed for 'Newcomers'." *The Mandate.* October 1985, p. 5.

Tutterow, Michael. "Southern Baptists Stress Language and Culture." *The Mandate.* October 1985, p. 8.

Weece, Roy. "Jesus Voted Yes!" *Christian Standard.* 26 July, 1987, pp. 1, 4-6.

Weece, Roy. "The Strangers." *Christian Standard.* 11 March 1984, pp. 19,20.

Westbury, Joe. "The Internationals: The Tourists." *MissionsUSA.* September-October 1987, pp. 9-15.

"Who Will Win America?" *MissionsUSA.* March/April 1987, pp. 4-9.

DATE DUE
